LOURDES FOR TODAY
AND
TOMORROW

JACQUES PERRIER

LOURDES FOR TODAY
AND
TOMORROW

New City - London / NDL éditions

First published in Great Britain by

New City
Unit 17, Sovereign Park
Coronation Road,
London NW10 7QP

©2008 New City, London

Translated by Sophie Rowe from the French *Lourdes Aujourd'hui, Et demain?*
© 2007, Nouvelle Cité,
Domaine d'Arny – Bruyères-le-Châte, France

Cover Design by Tomeu Mayans & Laurent Boudre
Pictures cover & back cover:
© Sanctuaires Notre-Dame de Lourdes/EURL Basilique Rosaire
Pictures accompanying the personal experiences inside the book:
© Nouvelle Cité/NDL éditions

British Cataloguing in Publication Data:
A catalogue reference for this book is available from the British Library

ISBN 978-1-905039-05-0

Typeset by New City
Printed and bound in Great Britain by Cromwell Press, Trowbrige, Wilstshire

CONTENTS

WHY THIS BOOK?

This book marks the 150th anniversary of the apparitions of the Blessed Virgin Mary to Bernadette Soubirous in 1858. Its title could have been, *Lourdes, Yesterday and Tomorrow*. Jubilee 2008 ought to commemorate the original event, but at the same time it should be open to new perspectives on the future.

In this respect, the Jubilee reflects the Centenary of 1958. Mgr Théas, Bishop of Tarbes and Lourdes at that time, wished to use the occasion to focus on the shrine of Lourdes, its origins, and history, but at the same time to prepare the shrine to better welcome the ever increasing multitudes of pilgrims who visited it each year.

Two great monuments remain from 1958: first, a documentary and critique, by Abbot Laurentin and Fr Billet; second, a monument of architecture, the Basilica of St Pius X, designated by the French Ministry of Culture as "A remarkable patrimony of the 20th Century". Fifty years later neither of these two monuments has been superseded.

Jubilee 2008 should serve to announce the Gospel at the outset of the third millennium. What contribution has Lourdes to offer to the Church's mission in our times? To find the answer we must both return to the source, but also take into account what has happened over 150 years and so identify those doorways to the Gospel that Lourdes is opening to our contemporaries. Certainly, our contemporaries are many and varied and the doorways are numerous: in this book we have named but twelve, a significantly apostolic number.

The following chapters each present one aspect of the Church's mission in which Lourdes has a certain amount of credibility and therefore responsibility.

Several of these aspects date back as far as Lourdes itself, and form the very heart of the message: Call to conversion and prayer; the Immaculate Conception; the Eucharist; the sick.

Others aspects have been added since: volunteers; young people; peace; the global perspective.

More recently, still others have been added, namely: ecumenism; political refugees; the mentally impaired; inter-religious dialogue.

Of all these aspects, Pope Benedict XVI had set three as "priorities":

1 The sick
In our world, which tries to hide or even eliminate suffering and which nevertheless has to face up to it every day without being able to find any sense in it, the problem of suffering is very important. It is an essential part of the mission of Lourdes. Moreover, the relationship between the problem of suffering and the passion of Christ allows us to demonstrate the centrality of Christology.

2 The Immaculate Conception and the Catholic faith vis-à-vis Mary

Lourdes is, above all, a Marian place and its mission is inseparably linked to the dogma of the Immaculate Conception. This dogma still poses difficulties due to the many misunderstandings; on the other hand, there is a new awareness among Christian people, of the place of Mary, also in the Protestant Churches. In order to develop a new Christian anthropology a glance in the direction of Mary opens up new perspectives.

3 The Eucharist and eucharistic adoration

Right from the beginning, Lourdes was never only a Marian place; it was always a eucharistic place. The centrality of the Eucharist in the Christian life was highlighted by Vatican II which defined this sacrament as "the source and summit of the Christian life" (Lumen Gentium, LG no 11). Pope John Paul II also appealed in many of his encyclicals and in particular in Ecclesia de Eucharistia, *that "The Church draws her life from the Eucharist. This truth does not simply express a daily experience of faith, but recapitulates the heart of the mystery of the Church" (LG no 1). "In recent times, a unilateral vision of the Eucharist had obscured the significance of Eucharistic adoration. Today we see more clearly that adoration is a fundamental aspect of the act of communion, of the "shared bread"; it is the personalisation of the sacramental act: sacramental devotion and personal devotion go together. In the wake of the later documents of Pope John Paul II, I believe that we have to work to highlight this synthesis of the different aspects of the Eucharist."*

(From a letter to the Bishop of Tarbes and Lourdes,
18 July 2005)

The story of Lourdes may be compared to that of a religious family. One must always return to the original charism in order to be faithful to that grace which God wishes it to give to our times, not merely repeat mechanically their deeds and habits, for repetition is but laziness, whereas faithfulness is inventive.

In each chapter we will ask how a particular aspect of the Church's mission first emerged at Lourdes, how it developed, what contribution Lourdes now offers and how to go ahead.

But the reader must not take this the wrong way: Lourdes does not in any way seek to preach to others. It does not claim to be the finest flower of the Church. However, as with all religions, we know that pilgrimages and shrines play an ever-increasing role. Lourdes simply wishes to integrate itself more fully with the mission of the Church and to serve in accordance with its charism.

In this way Lourdes can call itself a Marian shrine, to be as Mary, "the handmaid of the Lord".

+Jacques Perrier
Bishop of Tarbes and Lourdes

Chapter One

THE MISSION OF THE CHURCH WITH VOLUNTEER WORKERS, FOR THE SERVICE OF OTHERS

The backdrop

Nowadays we attach considerable importance to humanitarian aid. Occasionally we read about such organisations being disbanded because they had grown too large, or about the misappropriation of funds and so-called "business-charities".

However, to see things in this way is to get things out of proportion. Vigilance and critical discernment are to be welcomed, but they must not become an alibi for what old-fashioned morality would call 'egoism' and 'greed'.

Voluntary service and humanitarianism must not be confused. I would imagine that those who volunteer their help for the charity "Médecins du Monde" are paid; but that does not mean that they do not put themselves at great personal risk to go to the most desperate areas. Nor is it forbidden for a policeman or security guard to have altruistic motives. As for the president of an association of stamp collectors, it may be that he dedicates considerable time to fulfilling his responsibility, without getting paid. His stamp collection, however, is not directly humanitarian.

Although it is necessary to make this distinction, voluntary work and humanitarian activity usually overlap. Let us return to our stamp collector. This man could preoccupy himself with nothing but his collection and spend hours on the Internet researching a very rare stamp. In accepting his responsibility as president of an association, he is aware that he must listen to others, propose decisions which may be contrary to their opinions, collect together only a few in order to document his decisions once they have been adopted by the general assembly. Even if the association is modest in size, all of this represents a considerable amount of work. For the benefit of the members of the association who do not realise this, he is indirectly fulfilling a humanitarian role.

With the crumbling of the family unit and the weakening of relations at work or in the neighbourhood, western society would be far worse off if it wasn't for all the associations animated by volunteers. In the 30 – 50 age range many would rather be members of sports clubs, or parent-pupil and other local associations. In the more mature age group, who are less tied down by immediate obligations, many will belong to humanitarian associations: it is easier to distribute meals to the hungry when you have a little spare time on your hands. Many of them will engage in religious activities, even though these may not strictly be called associations as such. Can all of this activity be called humanitarian? My reply is "yes". To look after a dozen children in a catechism class is doubly humanitarian: the children are being cared for, but their faith, which deepens our humanity, is being nurtured.

Being a volunteer is therefore complex. Each person will have their own motives for doing something. In the aftermath of the Second World War, the Catholic Church in France became involved in the world of work specifically through Catholic Action, working priests, and la "Mission de France". So it is a very sensible question to put to ourselves today: what is the Church's mission with regard to volunteer workers? Perhaps Lourdes has something to say on this matter?

Lourdes: miracles and shopkeepers

This, I think would be the definition of Lourdes for many who have never been there. We will say more about miracles with regard to the sick. As for the shopkeepers, they are no more numerous than anywhere else, if we take into account the 6 million visitors every year. They are simply more apparent because they are concentrated in the only two streets which lead to the shrine. Whilst that may seem to let them off the hook somewhat, it is nonetheless true that Lourdes is much more a city of volunteer workers than of shopkeepers.

"Hospitality" is a key-note in Lourdes. Hospitality is as old as the Bible itself, perhaps even as old as humanity itself: so many peoples witness it, in so many different ways.

In Scripture, the prototype of hospitality is the first of the patriarchs: Abraham. On seeing three men approaching in the heat of the noonday sun, so close to his tent, he hurries towards them and begs them stay and rest a while and share a meal with him. But this text from Genesis 28 is not simply a recommendation for us on how to behave. These three passers-by, to whom Scripture refers sometimes in the singular, sometimes in the plural, are God himself who has come to visit Abraham and to promise him a descendency beyond anything he would have ever dared hope for. Hospitality, emblem of the Christian, has, therefore a theological dimension. "Whatever you did to the least of my brothers, you did to me." "Whoever welcomes you, welcomes me." Whoever welcomes a brother is, in fact, visited by God, and the relationship of generosity is reversed: the one who welcomes receives more than he gave because he receives that which only God can give.

When the pilgrims came to Lourdes in the middle of the 19th century, had they read the book of Genesis? We can't be sure, and yet it is quite possible, because knowledge of sacred history was far more widespread than we may imagine, we who are left to dissect the texts. But let us move on. That is another matter.

If the pilgrims of the 19th century were not directly inspired by Abraham, they were not lacking in examples of hospitality among the saints through the ages and from religious congregations. In the 4th century, Basil, bishop of Cesarea, had built a hospital in his hometown. How many holy queens have given their personal gifts (or those of their royal husbands) to help the poor. Those travellers who ventured to cross the Alps were blessed when they came across the followers of St Bernard and heard the bells as night fell, giving direction to their steps.

As for religious congregations, founded on the ransom of captives, help to the needy, care of the sick, they are countless. During the 19th century they came to life in diocese after diocese. But the Sisters of Charity and Christian Instruction of Nevers date back to 1680. They had been present in Lourdes since 1834. It was with them that Bernadette was to find refuge after her apparitions and to find her religious vocation of service to the poor.

The volunteers of the Our Lady of Lourdes Centre for Hospitality

Until recently, we have been used to referring to the men and women volunteers separately , for the simple reason that, traditionally, they performed different tasks.

But let us go back to the days immediately following the apparitions. Already during the apparitions many were flocking to Lourdes, some to pray, some to find proof that it was all a hoax. From 1st march 1858, Lourdes revealed its own particular charism. That night, Catherine Latapie came from Loubajac to pray at the Grotto. She plunged her withered hand into the stream which had only been flowing for three days. Catherine was cured and since that night the sick have never ceased to come to Lourdes in the hope of a cure and in the certainty of being comforted.

Whilst the able-bodied pilgrims organised themselves and found lodging as best they could, it was essential to think about who could accompany the sick? And since they often came from far away, how would they be received and looked after when thy got there? Buildings went up both close to the shrine itself and nearby. The first to be built was in 1874. Once the Hospice of the Sisters of Nevers, now the Municipal Hospital, it cared for the very first sick pilgrims who came to Lourdes.

But not only buildings were needed: who was going to look after those wishing to come to Lourdes but unable to come on their own? The sisters set to work: the Little Sisters of the Assumption, the Sisters of Our Lady of Sorrows (Mary-Saint-Frai), the Sisters of Nevers. But even their help was not enough for the task involved. They could welcome the sick once in Lourdes but how would they get back home again?

And so the hospitality centres and teams came into being: the Hospitality Centre of Our Lady of Good Health for the national pilgrimages from 1881 onwards, succeeded by the Hospitality Centre of Our Lady of Lourdes and the Hospitality Teams for the Diocesan and National Pilgrimages. The Our Lady of Lourdes Hospitality Centre is international

17

and the hospitality teams exist in every country which sends sick people to Lourdes.

Helpers are aged 18 and over and in total there are about 100,000 of them. At their own expense they give up one week every year to care for the sick. The women often wear a veil, which given the setting, can mean that they are mistaken for nuns, but which are in fact more like a nurse's veil. The men, who in the old days would have worn shoulder straps useful for the carrying of stretchers, now wear reflective jackets so they are clearly visible when they need to direct the movement of pilgrims or maintain a degree of silence around the Grotto.

The men and women helpers are not the only volunteers at Lourdes. We must not forget:

– those who assist with each individual pilgrimage.

– the priests who come to help, especially with the sacrament of reconciliation.

– the Helpers of the city of St Pierre, founded by Mgr Rodhain in 1955.

– the seminarians from various nations who during the summer put themselves at the service of the pilgrims for a fortnight.

– the young people who in a special way look after the "Village for Youth".

– the medical service provided by doctors and nurses.

– the workers of St-Martin, the halls of residence, the "Welcome and Listen" help point.

– the stewards responsible for guiding pilgrims who are not sure how to find their way around the vast areas of the shrine.

– the Handicapped Children's Pilgrimage Trust (HCPT).

And so many others who almost anonymously give their support in one or other of the services provided at the shrine.

A few humanitarian organisations have calculated in financial terms what the corresponding cost would be of paying for the work that is carried out by volunteers. We have not done this calculation – the figures would be astronomical. But we have not done it for other reasons, because Lourdes, without its volunteers, would be inconceivable. At Lourdes we are not talking about helpers assisting the professionals. It is the professionals who must allow the helpers to fulfil their mission, the pilgrims to make their journey, and the visitors to understand that Lourdes is not a theme park.

A Christian spirituality of service

In his encyclical *God is Love* Pope Benedict XVI makes a specific reference to voluntary service. (nos. 30- 31) Initially he refers simply to the "emergence and expansion of the various forms of voluntary service, which cover a wide range of services". Even when there is no religious connection, these initiatives are actively promoting what John Paul II calls "a culture of life" as opposed to "a culture of death". The Pope goes on to say that voluntary humanitarian activity is a favourable terrain for ecumenical activity.

Nevertheless the question inevitably arises: what conditions are necessary to safeguard the "charitable work of the Church" against becoming a variation of organised social work? The Pope notes three such conditions.

– Do not rely solely on professional competence, though this is certainly important in the type of work we are doing. Never forget that human beings need the "warmth of our hearts". It is therefore necessary that Christian volunteers should acquire a "training of the heart". Those who are responsible for the activities carried out need to "guide the volunteers to a meeting with God in Christ, which enkindles this love, and enables them to open their spirit to others."

– Be free with regard to every ideology. What matters is to "do good, now, personally, passionately, wherever possible, independently of strategies and party politics. The Christian programme is the programme of the Good Samaritan, of Jesus. It is "seeing" with the heart.

– Charitable action must be unpaid. By its very nature, love is the best witness we can give to God, the "God in whom we believe". "The Christian knows when it is the moment to speak of God and when it best to stay silent and let love speak": that does not mean that we exclude him, for "often it is precisely the absence of God that is the deepest root of suffering".

Are these three characteristics outlined by the Pope exclusively Christian? Certainly not. The "attention of the heart", the warmth of love, a heart which "sees", without payment, these are not exclusively Christian characteristics. Yet, without them, true Christian charity cannot exist. Faith in Christ, therefore, helps to give value to these aspects of voluntary humanitarian service which might otherwise end up devoid of human qualities.

Generosity dwells naturally in the heart of each and every person created in the image and likeness of God who is love. But a spiritual dimension is needed to prevent falling into the trap of self-satisfaction, or the lure of power under the guise of service, or of weariness. This dimension comes with faith, to all those who try to live out a Christian spirit of service. This is of benefit to the whole humanitarian movement.

Charity and voluntary work are often criticised from the point of view that they simply ease our conscience. I dedicate several hours or several days to the service of others but then the rest of the time I think only about my own interests, even to the detriment of others. And yet the opposite is also possible, and it is in this opposite direction that we should go:

voluntary activity should give me the desire to serve others, in all of my activities, in the family, at work or in my leisure time.

Pope Benedict XVI continues his reflection (nos. 36-39) by insisting on the role of prayer. In fact, throughout history the saints best known for their charitable activities were men and women of prayer: St Vincent de Paul, Father Joseph Wresinski, founder of ATD Fourth World, Mother Teresa. Prayer is a defence against becoming institutionalised, but it is also a defence against resignation or despair in the face of immense need. It can be a lament, like that of Job. But, finally, it leads us to humility, because it makes us realise that, happily, we are not omnipotent. Humility is another name for realism.

Speaking of serving others, the Pope offers perhaps the densest thought of his whole encyclical, "This task is a grace." Most volunteers, whatever their motivation would agree with the well known expression, "We received more than we gave." Ultimately, it is the task of the Church to show them that it is from God that this experience comes: "There is more joy in giving than in receiving," because giving is our vocation as human beings.

PERSONAL EXPERIENCE

Looking after the sick at Lourdes

If I look back over the last 5 years, I am able to see that it is Our Lady who places the most beautiful desires in our hearts, the desire to serve her, and to serve her pilgrims at Lourdes. I myself received the grace to serve even before I ever knew that one day I would visit the Grotto. As I took care first of my grandmother and then of my father, I was grateful to be able to take care of them, even though I am only a wife and mother, and not a nurse. It was a privilege for me to be able to serve them in their simplest needs. After their departure for the "next life" I wondered how I could continue to take care of others, as I didn't have any medical qualifications. I prayed to God and asked him to show me the way.

Shortly afterwards a friend of mine had her business card pulled out of a lottery. Her prize was 2 free plane tickets to Europe for the Jubilee Year. Without understanding what it meant to go on a pilgrimage, we decided, as Americans do, to make a tour of the holy places in Europe. It was while we were visiting these wonderful places, that I experienced a deep healing in Lourdes, a deep conversion as I entered the baths.

I remember thinking that if I ever had the opportunity to make another pilgrimage during my lifetime, I would love to come back here to such a holy place. Never for one moment did I imagine that I would be returning to Lourdes the following year once more on a free ticket! I can only say that my experience had been life-changing. When my husband came to collect me from the airport, he remarked, after 25 years of marriage, that he was collecting a new wife! – Something many husbands wish they could say!

So to my great astonishment, I returned to Lourdes a year later, with the free gift of a pilgrimage, this time to accompany two sick ladies. I was about to learn what it means to accompany and welcome others, two attitudes of service specific to Lourdes, almost unknown to Americans.

For four days we queued up in the morning, each time getting nearer to the entrance to the baths, but each time without actually being able to go inside – which was the main reason we had come to Lourdes! Then came the feast of the Ascension 2001 - a few years later I learnt that, in the history of Lourdes, that day has probably been the day that the greatest number of women tried to enter the baths. There were many sick people that day, and not very many helpers. At that time I thought that every person who wore a badge was a paid worker. First as a tourist, and now as a pilgrim, I saw this most beautiful of shrines filled with smiling people, each one helping others. I knew nothing about helpers, nor that these people wearing white uniforms were volunteers and not nurses. I began to worry that I was not going to be able to enter the baths. So I left the queue, giving my place to someone else, in the hope that they might be able to experience the same extraordinary blessing that I had received last year. Then I asked the gentleman who stood at the entrance to the baths, why we had not yet managed to get in. Straightaway he informed another lady who spoke English. She said I had a lovely genuine smile and asked me if I could touch my toes – I still can today!

Then she asked me to come in with her and help to bathe the sick and dying and she promised that the two women I had come with would be able to enter the baths. She led me inside, gave me an apron and sent me to pool no 4. To my great surprise those strong women who were helping, spoke neither English nor French, only Italian! What followed was a training session by example and sign language! It was a day of extraordinary blessings and witnesses of faith. Because I did not speak or understand Italian, the whole day was demanding and difficult. However, I was able to help about half of the English-speaking pilgrims. Serving others at the pool that day, helping all those grandmothers to enter the water, has been the greatest privilege of my life. It is through these smallest of gestures, discreet, simple and gentle, performed throughout the day, that we experience great joy. Praying with other women as we serve Christ in the way his mother, the Blessed Virgin Mary of the Grotto, wishes, draws us as close as we can get to experiencing that "other world". It is undoubtedly a gift to help so many women from all over the world and to pray with them in the universal language of Lourdes – our smile.

After this period of service, God placed the desire in my heart to promise Our Lady to return the following year with 10 more helpers, good Catholic women. That privilege was granted, only this time I paid for my own ticket! Serving others at the shrine has become the greatest experience of my life.

To serve alongside others brings with it moments of laughter and of tears, treasured memories and the gift of new friendships. I learn to love because Our Lady introduces me to all her friends! An unbreakable bond forms between us during that week of sacrifice and joy. It is a magnificent gift to meet up with other North Americans who have come to serve as men and women helpers. My husband and I are both grateful for this time of service to the Church. Does such an opportunity exist anywhere else? It is the love of our Mother, at the heart of the Welcome Centre, which makes us all one family living in true charity.

At Lourdes, we witness through serving that the Church is alive, and through the friendships we build each year, that it is universal. In serving Our Lady and her pilgrims, we are blessed with this unique opportunity to practise the works of mercy, both material and spiritual. A precious gift of our service is to be able to take home these moments and experiences full of charity to our families and parishes. It is impossible to leave behind the graces we have received. We must bring the gift of serving back home.

Marlene Watkins

CHAPTER TWO

THE MISSION OF THE CHURCH
AND MARY

One of the great contributions brought to the Church by the Second Vatican Council was its link with Mary. Should there have been a Council document dedicated to her alone? According to journalists there was an intense debate among the bishops about this.

Some were hoping for a document that would reflect and crown the intensity of Marian piety that had characterised the 19th and 20th centuries, in which the two dogmas had been declared: the Immaculate Conception in 1854, and the Assumption in 1950. Some thought that the Council might add to Mary's titles that of Co-Redemptress.

Other bishops, who eventually carried the motion, thought it was wiser not to speak about Mary as if she were divine or semi-divine, but, on the contrary, to bring her closer to us: of all creatures she is the most holy, but she is still a creature. As the mother of Jesus, she is the Mother of God, Theotokos, but she is not the mother of his divinity. This confusion or accusation caused great division in the Church during the 5th Century. It would have been pointless to start all over again 15 centuries later.

Instead, the Blessed Virgin Mary, Mother of God, in the mystery of Christ and of the Church, takes her place in the 8th and final chapter of *Lumen Gentium, Dogmatic Constitution of the Church*. In the preceding chapter, the Council looks at the Church's course through history and her union with the Church in heaven, of which Mary, through her Assumption, is rightly the first representative. The preface for that day's feast states clearly: "Today, the Virgin Mary, Mother of God, is taken up into the glory of heaven: perfect image of the Church to come, dawn of the Church triumphant, she guides and maintains the hope of your people still "on their way" or, as the original Latin said "on pilgrimage". This has a special connotation with regards to Lourdes.

Mary and the Church in Scripture and Tradition

The link between Mary and the Church is clear in St Luke and St John's Gospels.

St Luke draws a parallel between the Annunciation and Pentecost: through the Holy Spirit the Son of God is made flesh in the womb of the Virgin Mary. By the same spirit, the frightened group of disciples in the upper room becomes the Body of Christ, his Church. Mary is there, awaiting the coming of the Holy Spirit, but she is not a substitute for the Church. All were of one heart, praying earnestly together and a few of the women were among them, including Mary the mother of Jesus (Acts 1, 14). Mary is not at the centre, as she is often depicted at Pentecost, but she is present.

In St John's Gospel, the definitive moment for Mary is at the foot of the cross, when Jesus says "Behold your son" and to his beloved disciple, "Here is your mother" (John 19 26-27). "My mother and my disciples are those who hear the Word and put it into practice," said Jesus when his mother had come looking for him (Luke 8, 21). This new family is the Church, of whom Mary is the first representative.

As they sought to interpret the Old Testament, the Fathers of the Church asked themselves who the woman could be? Did she foretell Mary or the Church? They came to the conclusion that both interpretations were inseparably linked; neither excluded the other.

So too with Judith and Esther, the strong women who saved the people from mortal danger.

So too the "daughter of Sion", besieged by enemies, but through suffering, blessed with fruitfulness beyond compare, evokes both the figure of Mary, whose own heart, in the words of the prophet Simeon, would be pierced by a sword of sorrow, and also the Church, which at the end of time would be "blessed to have given so many sons and daughters (to the Father)" [from the preface of the Mass for the dedication of a church].

So too the spouse of the Song of Songs. When the lover sings of the beauty of his beloved, does he foretell Mary so splendid in grace, or the Church, for whom Christ sacrificed himself, so that she would be spotless, without wrinkle or any such thing, but holy and faultless (Ephesians 5, 27).

Scripture experts never cease to wonder who the woman of the Apocalypse is. Some characteristics evoke Mary in her glory, mother of he who is "the shepherd of all the nations"; other characteristics evoke the persecuted Church for whom the book of the Apocalypse was inspired.

Parallels

The close link between Mary and the Church seems therefore to be fully founded upon faith. But in what way does Mary's mission coincide with the Church's mission? It would be best to return to the teaching of Vatican II, to the chapter previously mentioned.

The Council recalls firstly the role that Mary played during the different stages of Jesus' life. Her importance is never in question but we must not forget that she, in her own words, calls herself handmaid of the Lord: "I am the handmaid of the Lord: let it be done to me according to your word" ; " He has looked upon his lowly handmaid," sings Mary in her Magnificat. To the servants at the wedding feast of Cana, she says: "Do whatever he tells you," pointing to Jesus. So it is with the Church: she points to Jesus. In fact, she gives Jesus through the announcement of the Word and through the sacraments. That is why we can call the Church, mother. Yet she does not substitute Christ. Since Vatican II, we have been used to using the same expression for the Church as for Mary: "lowly handmaid".

As well as the titles "handmaid" and "mother", also the name "virgin", is as appropriate for the Church as for Mary. "Imitating the mother of the Lord, and by virtue of the Holy Spirit, the Church safeguards in purest virginal state, an integral faith, a steadfast hope and sincere charity" (no. 64). In 1987 Pope John Paul II dedicated an encyclical to the Virgin Mary entitled *Redemptoris Mater*. Throughout her life Mary lived a pilgrimage of faith. The Pope meditates upon the words of Elizabeth: "Blessed is she who believed." Mary's faith had to pass through many trials before she entered into the clear vision of the kingdom of heaven. From the very beginning she had complete faith, but it is

30

also true to say that her faith increased right up to the moment of the cross.

In the same way, the Church is on a pilgrimage of faith. She encounters many trials; that is particularly true today in our own countries. On the day of Pentecost the Church's faith is complete. But it is also true to say that her faith increases through the many expressions of sanctity that the Holy Spirit brings to life through the ages, especially that of the martyrs.

Our Lady of Lourdes: a model for the Church

What has been said so far applies to every place where Mary is venerated. What we need to do now is understand the message of Mary as she originally manifested herself in Lourdes; how it outlines the mission of the Church, in the spirit of the Second Vatican Council and for our times.

The 18 apparitions constitute a true Christian initiation. After the time of instruction comes the moment of invitation to personal prayer from Mary to Bernadette, and the moment of trust. The 8th to the 12th apparition is the moment of penance. Bernadette is then entrusted with a mission for the Church; she goes to ask the priest to build a chapel and to organise processions. The name of the lady is only revealed later. Then silence descends once again, until the 16 July, when Bernadette sees the Virgin from a distance, more beautiful than ever, but for the last time, as she intuitively understands. This initiation begins during Lent with the miracle of the candle on 4 April. The initiation consists of words, silences, absences, gestures, support but also trials, and a mission. Mary's instruction is an excellent model for the Church which is entrusted with the initiation of a living faith.

At Lourdes, Mary never puts herself on a pedestal. When the beads of her rosary slip through her fingers, her lips do not move, except at the end of the decade when Bernadette recites: "Glory be to the Father and to the Son and to the Holy Spirit." Bernadette had returned to Lourdes from Bartrès in order to make her First Holy Communion which took place on 3 June. It was Mary who led Bernadette to the Eucharist. This is how it is in Lourdes. People may criticise the fact that there are so many altars in the grotto, insisting that in Christian spirituality the Eucharist must come first. But in the same way the niche where the Virgin appeared is distinct from the spring. Mary points to the spring, but she herself is not the spring. St Bernard described her as the "channel". All of this applies rigorously to the Church in her mission of evangelisation.

The Lady took on the smallness in stature of Bernadette. And she is so young. Above all, she speaks Bernadette's language. It was because of difficulties with language that Bernadette found it so hard to keep up with the catechism, and the reason why she had been held back from making her First Communion which she longed for so much. The Virgin Mary did not attend the Second Vatican council to "inculturate herself". Speaking of language, Bernadette has a disarming reply. To someone who strongly doubted that anyone acting on God's behalf would understand the local dialect, she said: "But how would we be able to understand it if God doesn't understand it?"

The great originality of Lourdes, lies in the Lady's name, which she revealed on the feast of the Annunciation: "I am the Immaculate Conception." The angel's words were: "Rejoice, you who are full of grace." Even more powerfully then, do we speak of Mary as "work of grace".

Because she is all grace. Mary, like her Son, welcomes sinners. Sinners will deceive and fight each other. But Mary is the "refuge of sinners". For centuries we have entreated her: "Pray for us poor sinners." Jesus says: "Go, and sin no more." Mary tells sinners what she told the servants at Cana: "Do whatever he tells you."

Despite our sins, the Church is "holy", as Mary is immaculate. In particular she welcomes sinners in the sacrament of reconciliation. She does not turn her gaze from difficult situations but in a special way she recognises suffering and openness of heart, lived by those who find themselves in those situations. Lourdes offers many different ways in which we may express our sincere desire for conversion, even outside of the sacrament of reconciliation.

Nothing escapes her grace; she is available for the needs of each and every person. She is all welcome. She is the perfect mother. This is the experience of millions and millions of pilgrims each year. Jesus said: "Whatever you did to the least, you did it to me." What would a mother not do for her child? Mary's love for Jesus extends to the smallest and least of his little ones, the sick and the marginalised. This is the path which the Church must follow.

The Visitation

The Church's mission is to welcome and initiate. But more precisely it is to announce the good news of the Gospel to those who have not heard it. "Go therefore and make disciples of all nations," is Jesus' command after the Resurrection. "We have come to proclaim," says Paul, "that which no eye has seen, no ear has heard, no mind has visualised" (1 Corinthians, 2, 9).

Faith comes from the message. But there is no message without a messenger, no messenger unless he is sent. (Romans 10, 14-17). If not, he would merely be speaking on his own account, and his words would not be worth more than himself. Jesus, on the other hand, is sent by the Father, and in his turn he sends his disciples. This is "mission" in its strictest sense.

The Fathers recount that it was the women who were the first to carry the message on the morning of the Resurrection. Before them, Mary had been the first messenger of the Gospel at the moment of the Visitation. Mary is young. She bears within her the one who is radically new. She goes to visit her older cousin Elizabeth who bears within her the one who is to be his precursor. Elizabeth was expecting a baby, but like all devout Jews, even more she was awaiting the liberation of Israel. Who would this liberator be? She did not know. But when Mary greets her, the child in her womb leaps for joy and she recognises in Mary the mother of the Lord. Full of awe she rejoices: "Why should I be honoured by a visit from the mother of my Lord" (Luke 1, 43).

The Visitation is the most perfect example of mission, in accordance with the spirit of Second Vatican Council. Mary's visit fulfils Elizabeth's waiting, who like Simeon in his old age "awaited the consolation of Israel" (Luke 2, 25). But her visit is also filled with surprise. As much as it awakens Elizabeth's joy, it awakens Mary's joy as she then sings in her Magnificat.

Israel's waiting, as told over and over again by the prophets, is original. But as Vatican II, and the Greek Fathers, remind us, every individual created in the image and likeness of God, awaits his salvation. For the pagan, conversion lies in recognising Christ as the one he is waiting for.

Can we not compare the authentic apparitions of Mary at Lourdes and elsewhere to the Visitation? Without doubt the Visitation is unique. Elizabeth and John the Baptist are unique in the history of salvation. The revelation of the Gospel is achieved, but not its diffusion. In order to communicate the Gospel today, God continues to take the initiative through the Holy Spirit who animates the Church, but who first of all animates Mary who is the Church personified and perfect. Just as she went to visit Elizabeth, she went to visit Bernadette. She fulfilled her desire to be in communion with Christ.

In the same way, the mission of the Church is to go out to meet all people to announce the Gospel and to fulfil their deepest longings.

Mary

My name is Régine-Marie and I come from Finistère where my parents owned a small grocery store which was a popular meeting place for young people. As a child I was so naughty that I made life impossible for my parents. All the same I always believed in family values and in friendship. I never hesitated to go miles to help a friend in need. Brought up by the sea, I was very independent, with a taste for risk and adventure. I would go on long solitary walks along the wild coast drawing strength from the sound of the waves, the cry of the sea gulls and the wind. What could be more beautiful than the sunset over the sea? It was enough for me to contemplate it without any words to feel my whole being filled with calm.

As a child, religion meant nothing to me. I could not see a difference between someone who was practising and someone who wasn't. In Brittany it is customary to say the rosary but I didn't take kindly to that at all because it didn't mean anything to me. What was the point of this devotion to Mary? OK she may be Jesus' mother but how did that make her mine?

I was 16 when my parents won a ticket to Lourdes on the diocesan pilgrimage. No one in my family wanted to go, so my mother convinced me to at least go as a tourist once in my life. I went with a group of young people from my locality. I tried to run off whenever they prayed too much. However, I was attracted to the grotto and went there of my own accord. One morning, some of us decided to go to Mass at 5.30 a.m. in the Grotto. I was the first to get up and go. At a certain moment, I gazed at the statue of Mary and these words came to my lips: "I want to give you my whole life because I want to be like you." I was amazed at my own words - that was my first flash of lightning. After Mass I did the Way of the Cross on my knees. I did it more for my family and my friends than for myself. I placed before Jesus all those who had requested me to think of them and who would have liked to be present at Lourdes. Jesus, who up until then had meant nothing to me, began to speak to me more and more.

At the end of that summer I started my training as a bus driver. More than 1000 boys attended the technical college of whom about 100 were in the transport department and I was the only girl. My mechanics teacher was a member of a religious order. He had a way of listening to us and explaining the lesson to us in such a way that it was almost impossible not to understand. One day, he left a piece of paper on top of my tool box and said he was available any time to discuss it with me. It was the Word of Life (a sentence from the Scripture with a commentary by Chiara Lubich, founder and president of the Focolare Movement, distributed to thousands of people throughout the world). We talked for over an hour, during which time he spoke to me about Mary. From that moment, her maternity remained engraved on my soul. He revealed a Mary who was close to me in my everyday life. I left his office and cried for most of the rest of the evening, I don't even know why because I wasn't sad!

Four days later this teacher invited me to an international festival of young people in Rome. I accepted straight away. There were about 50,000 young people in the stadium. As soon as what seemed to me a small, slight, woman arrived on the stage, these thousands of young people fell silent in order to listen to her with great attention. I was very impressed. I did not understand what she was saying in Italian, but I caught a glimpse. I saw in her another little Mary and a certainty invaded me, "She is the one I will follow," I said to myself.

Coming home was a big anti-climax. I had had such a strong experience in Rome. 50,000 young people in a stadium in which we had all shared the Ideal that it is possible to live the Gospel in depth. Now, in everyday life, this unity was a utopia. I found a job delivering fresh food to shops before they opened. On my twentieth birthday, as I prepared an order for delivery, a drunk man climbed into my lorry. I had just enough time to hide behind the milk crates and I had a metal bar in my hands, ready to hit him as hard as I could if he found me. At that moment I murmured the first part of the "Hail Mary" and the man turned on his heels and fled. I burst into tears crying, "Mary, what do you want from me?" A few weeks later I did not renew my contract and I found a job in the restaurant of a home for the elderly.

After these flashes of lightning with Mary, I went back to the church and the sacraments. Seeing me change, my father questioned me and I told him about my discovery of God as Love. He confided in me his own personal doubts and uncertainties and after years of searching he found God.

Some time later, I was invited to spend an evening in a Focolare. I remember two of Jesus' words that were mentioned that evening: "No one has greater love than he who lays down his life for his friends," and "Whoever does not leave father, mother, fields in order to follow me…" God was clearly speaking to me personally. I was perturbed, but I could not refuse his love, I couldn't give him less than my life. I found myself like Mary, with the possibility of saying "no", but I chose to say "yes" and to let him take possession of my life. That is how I came to enter the Focolare. My adventure with Mary continues today: she has led me to Jesus. Everyday I experience her maternity in the relationships I build, in my community, in my family, at work with my colleagues. "To be another little Mary," this is my programme for life, ambitious of course, but possible with the help of those near to me.

Régine-Marie Peron

CHAPTER THREE

THE MISSION OF THE CHURCH
AND YOUNG PEOPLE

A legitimate concern

Society is very much preoccupied with the young, and not only with those from inner city areas. At times violent, their actions can be hard to understand. It is not clear whether it is the young who refuse to integrate with society, leaving an irreparable rift, or whether it is society's failure to integrate with the young that drives them to such frustration.

The riots in Paris in the autumn of 1995 sent shock waves through French society. This was not just because of the fear they generated, but it was also the realization that the extreme behaviour of a small minority actually represented the discontent of many others.

Parents and grand-parents tend to think that things will be harder for their children: less pay, longer hours, more job insecurity, a damaged environment, a more uncertain world in which to live. Were previous generations just as sceptical? Between the wars some parents hesitated about having children at all: with the horror of the previous war still in their memories and fearing that another war was imminent, they rejected the possibility of generating "cannon fodder". However, over the last 2 or 3 centuries, people generally have believed that life would in fact improve from one generation to the next, given that progress looked set to continue, except in the event of temporary catastrophes such as war. This favourable view is no longer held today.

If adults worry all the time, young people are bound to respond negatively. It is not right to paint such a black picture. Many young people are content. Yet there is uncertainty everywhere. What studies to pursue? Which profession or job to choose? Why be committed to someone for ever when the divorce rate is so high? This uncertainty doesn't mean that we can't get on and live from day to day, but it makes long-term plans more difficult.

It seems that society has good reason therefore to be concerned about the young. However, since it does not have any solutions to offer, it prefers not to think too hard about the matter. From time to time we hear a politician eloquently ask the question "What sort of future are we preparing for our young people?" or "What world are we bequeathing to our children?" In the meantime things continue to get worse.

One section of society that always thinks about young people is the Church. Scarcely a meeting takes place within a parish or movement without someone asking, "Where are the young people?" At every diocesan synod there is always a sub-committee to report on the young with subsequent resolutions to be taken. When the annual reports relating to religious activities are drawn up, journalists, at least, are happy if they can say, "There were plenty of young people". But it's not enough just to be able to say, "There were plenty of young people". "Retired" celebrities can say they were happy that lots of young people came to their concerts. But this may not change very much.

Young people and Lourdes

When we think of Lourdes we think of the sick. This is perfectly understandable. For Lourdes, it is a privilege to welcome the sick with the greatest care, whatever their state of health, whatever distance travelled. Jesus was surrounded daily by the sick. Their constant presence in Lourdes, therefore, is in line with the Gospel.

The sick will always be the most important visitors to Lourdes, but today young people are also present in large numbers.

When did this begin? Right from the start. Bernadette and her companions were young. Our Lady appeared to Bernadette as a young girl, about the same age and height. The story of Lourdes began with these "Children of Mary" and their "torchlight processions". They would leave their parish church carrying candles to go and pray at the grotto and return still carrying them and singing psalms until they reached home.

Half a century later, in 1908, a group known as "Le Fraternel" began in Paris. In 1931, Catholic Action held its first national youth congress and pilgrimage in Lourdes with over 15,000 participants. The same year, 6000 Belgian Young Christian Workers gathered together with their founder Cannon Cardyn. Following their example, Mademoiselle Monnet, took up the same initiative with young people from more affluent backgrounds, known as the JIC (Jeunesse indépendante chrétienne). I have in front of me a photo from 1943 of the youth pilgrimage from the Bigorre region – there were at least 1000 present.

Lourdes wants to actively encourage young people to come. In 1935 the bishop bought a piece of land close to the Way of the Cross (Espélugues) and put it at the disposition of the Scouts of France. In the 1950s, Pierre Astruc, a member of the general commission for the Scouts of France, looked after the youth camp. Scouts had priority, but young people from other movements were also welcome when there was room.

From 1952 onwards, the French army used the camp for their national annual pilgrimage and it is thanks to their resources that the camp is well equipped. Many were doing military service, and this greatly added to the presence of young people in Lourdes.

It took a little time for the other pilgrimages to get used to so many younger pilgrims. Father Joudandet, Oblate of Mary Immaculate and chaplain of Lourdes, comments in 1961, how he wishes that people would stop referring to young people as though they were a "devastating cyclone".

The real commitment of Lourdes towards the young came in the 1970s. The big sign saying "Scout Reception" was changed to "Youth Reception". A year later a plot of land was found a little further out on the other side of the river Gave where the first roundhouse was built specifically for young people. The following year a second roundhouse was built and Mass was celebrated there every Saturday evening. In 1977, a priest from the diocese of Tarbes and Lourdes, André Cabes, was officially appointed to the shrine to look after young people. The celebration of youth Masses began, initially in a big marquee, and continues today in the church of St Bernadette. In 1985 the Oblates of Mary Immaculate came to help permanently.

Since then, tens of thousands of young people visit Lourdes every year. Only a small proportion can be put up at the *Cité S. Pierre* (youth village), but the Youth Welcome Centres are at the service of all young people who come, whether in groups or on their own. What is being offered to them is no less than what is being offered to every pilgrim: the opportunity to discover Lourdes, to pray at the Grotto, time for reflection, celebrations, processions, the way of the cross, the waters of the spring. Of course the style, language, rhythm and music are adapted according to age.

What is the secret of Lourdes' success regarding young people? Can it be defined and are there lessons to be drawn from it?

Why do young people like coming to Lourdes?

In Lourdes, you can take your time. Young people, like adults, can suffer from stress, perhaps even more acutely. The fast moving pace of life, the build up of images, emotions and information overload can all cause stress. In this hubbub, everything is designed to stimulate a reaction, never to reflect. To reflect and to be yourself, time out is needed, to give everything bubbling on the surface a chance to calm down. Young people find this time when they come to Lourdes, just as they do when they go to Taizé or participate in World Youth Days.

Nowadays the general ambience and conversation is so far removed, if not hostile to Christian faith, that it is first necessary to create the conditions which can allow people to actually hear the message of the Gospel.

Young people need people to talk to, and with whom they can experience even just a little of what it means to live a Christian life, a life of Christian community.

These things are not unique to Lourdes or young people

45

– we all need them. This is a key role that pilgrimages can fulfil whatever the religion. In a world ruled by money, profit, consumerism, and self-gratification, we have to provide the means for a spiritual life. A retreat in a monastery is one way, limited to a small number; a pilgrimage, or something similar, is another way, accessible to many.

A pilgrimage brings out the spiritual dimension within each person, allowing them to recognise their vocation as a child of God. During the pilgrimage, each person is free to express their faith, free to pray, when normally it is so hard to snatch even a few minutes for prayer or a brief 40 minutes to go to Mass on Sunday. People who never go to Mass at home, find it perfectly natural to attend daily Mass when they are in Lourdes.

Let us consider some other reasons why young people come to Lourdes, without trying to generalise too much, as young people would rather keep their own individuality than be stereo-typed.

They love witnesses. Bernadette is a witness who speaks to them. She was their age or a little bit younger, yet she behaves with great maturity. Without trying to act like an adult herself, she responds very bravely to them, some of them are extremely hostile, others dangerously deceitful or flattering towards her in order to get a favour. Bernadette's difficulties, her poor health and her lack of education, inspire confidence among the young: social ranking is not a necessary condition to be a person in your own right. How do they see Mary? I think that many would find it difficult to put their relationship with her into words. They are attracted by what Bernadette says: "The Lady spoke to me as one person speaks to another." The Blessed Virgin takes Bernadette seriously. She 'respects' her, a key word nowadays. She speaks to her with great delicacy: "Would you be so kind as to ..." Her messages are brief. Bernadette only needs a few words to convey them and this is very much a point in Mary's favour: young people do not appreciate long speeches. Often they do not believe them. They feel more comfortable with a presence. Mary is a friend they can trust. That is perhaps why the silent prayer at the Grotto is their strongest memory and impression of Lourdes.

Young people are also very keen to serve. Lourdes offers numerous possibilities, at the Welcome Centres and in other ways. Let's not forget the role that the Scouts played in the history of Lourdes. Service is part of the Scout ideal. Unfortunately, the activities of younger children, unless accompanied by an adult, are much restricted because of the regulations. Serving others leads us in the way of Christ, the servant par excellence: "I have come not to be served but to serve". Mary too declared herself the "handmaid" of the Lord. The fundamental question, therefore, is how to give service its true Christian dimension? It is serving that opens our hearts and makes us available to others.

Lourdes has another advantage and that is space. Many things can go on at the same time without disturbing others. This means that young people can have their own special time, not only in the youth village, out of the way, but also at the shrine, and they can also spend time together with all the other pilgrims. They do not lead separate lives, but neither are they swallowed up in a big crowd. It works in the same way at world youth meetings: large numbers of adults accompany the young, and parishes and families take them and spend time with them. They are not left "on their own". In Taizé the main focus of adult attention is the Community of Brothers. Naturally young people desire a certain amount of autonomy, but autonomy is not segregation.

In conclusion, Lourdes has an international and social dimension which goes beyond background and language. Young people are happy because they are widening their horizons despite the language barrier.

Lourdes offers all the elements which make it possible for young people to experience a Christian way of life anywhere. If visiting Lourdes can enhance many initiatives for and with young people, the shrine will have fulfilled its mission of service, and imitated Mary.

PERSONAL EXPERIENCE

Studying at the school of the Immaculate Conception

For as long as I can remember, I grew up beneath Mary's gaze. My parents brought me up as a Christian, and in particular with a special love for Our Lady of Lourdes. My mother was born on 11 February 1958 exactly one hundred years after the first apparition... maybe it was a sign.

I am from the diocese of Tarbes and Lourdes. The very first time I served at Mass was in Lourdes. I went to youth camps and retreats, as well as bigger gatherings. My faith was founded on Lourdes. I had been baptised in the School of Mary, nothing more, nothing less, it was all there.

Today I am 22, a 4th year student at university in Bordeaux. My course is in international relations. When dealing with questions of government and European integration I often draw from this school of love. In fact, it's quite funny: during my first year at Bordeaux I remember being asked a question during an oral exam which concerned the Immaculate Conception. I felt proud and happy to answer it.

I wasn't homesick at all! It was as though Our Lady was winking at me from up there! When you love Our Lady of Lourdes it's the same wherever you are – she watches over you in your everyday life.

Even while studying in Bordeaux I had many opportunities to go to Lourdes for both personal and collective prayer. Each time I passed through the grotto, or hugged and leant upon the rock, recited the rosary, joined in the torchlight procession, attended different pilgrimages, carried stretchers, it was though I had been freely given the tools to love. I remember a particular moment which made me understand the grace of Lourdes more deeply: during the Bigorre diocesan pilgrimage I had the joy of serving at Mass and accompanying the priests as they administered the sacrament of the sick on the meadow opposite the grotto. Outwardly that may not seem anything unusual as it is very normal to distribute the sacraments on such a big scale, but that day I was touched to the core by the presence of all these sick people, who were being given the sacrament with a love and intensity that cannot be put into words nor comprehended with our minds. When Mary instructed Bernadette to come here on pilgrimage, there was a grace attached that reaches into your innermost being and transforms you.

Another big moment for me was the visit of Pope John-Paul II in 2004. I was by his side with other young people from my diocese as he prayed the rosary. It was an unforgettable and decisive moment for me. The way in which he lived and spoke about the way of Mary, the way he prayed, and his words of encouragement and responsibility to us young people in that holy place, resounded within me, giving me the desire to commit myself more deeply to the life and service of the Church.

How many graces I and my friends received, how many

long hours of adoration… how many precious moments, such as when we sung chants through the streets of Lourdes one night in 2005, finishing in silence before the grotto late into the night.

Today, I am a member of the Emmanuel Community and I look after a prayer group of young people aged between 18 – 25 years. For the last two years we have held our annual youth camps at Lourdes. In 2007 we had the theme: "Set out! Commit yourself to the school of Mary". What a school!

Last year, surrounded by friends and family, I made my promise of commitment in front of the Grotto. Mary is at the centre of all my decisions. I cannot by-pass her!

I like to think of Lourdes as a seed of eternity which, starting with Bernadette, has implanted itself within us to guide us along paths of light and sanctity. Its school of love is so accessible that Mary herself comes to teach us humility and intimacy of heart. Its stream of pure water never ceases to flow through our daily lives, through our joys and sorrows, making God incarnate in our lives. Its grotto imprints itself on our hearts where, in welcoming Mary we welcome our salvation… Not so ordinary after all - a school of sanctity.

Anthony Lavardez

CHAPTER FOUR

THE MISSION OF THE CHURCH AND CHRISTIAN UNITY

It was during the 19th century that a Swiss Reformed Christian who had fallen in love with the Pyrenees came to settle at Baguères in the Bigorre region, where he built their first Protestant church. Evidence shows that at the time, there were two Protestant families living in Lourdes.

As for ecumenism, the word was unheard of in Bernadette's time. It was not to come about until much later, on the Protestant side with the Council of Edinburgh (1921) and, on the Catholic side, with Abbot Couturier (1881-1953) and the Week of Prayer for Christian Unity. Before these events, both sides remained in mutual ignorance and condemnation.

Given that it took place in such a context, how can the phenomenon of Lourdes have any part to play in today's ecumenical dialogue?

Lourdes from the Protestant viewpoint

There are many things in Lourdes that Christians from the Protestant tradition might find difficult. Firstly, the apparitions and their message would seem to go against the principle of *sola scriptura* (Scripture alone), namely that the whole of revelation is contained in the person of Christ and in the writings of the apostles; after that we have merely commentaries and interpretations determined by circumstance and culture.

Secondly, the Reformed Church tradition moved away from the mediaeval practice of pilgrimages and the veneration of saints. Pilgrimages and the popular belief of obtaining indulgences would seem to go against the principle of *sola gratia* (grace alone); and devotion to the saints would seem to go against the principle of one divine sanctity, attainable only through faith (*sola fides*).

Although these three principles, s*ola scriptura, sola gratia* and *sola fides* belong specifically to Calvin's teaching, they underlie the whole Reformation tradition. Perhaps most difficult of all from the Protestant viewpoint, might be the dogma of the Immaculate Conception, the continual stream of Masses and the entire ecclesial framework?

All this might lead us to the conclusion that Lourdes and the Reformed Church tradition are incompatible with one another. Happily this is not true. In the first place, how can any Christian of whatever persuasion resist being drawn to Bernadette?

Bernadette is undeniably Christian, with many typical traits: poverty, truth, humility, the desire to serve others, self-sacrifice, communion with the passion of Christ. Nothing spoke more of her total simplicity than Bernadette's own words and actions. She repeated often: "If there had been anyone in Lourdes poorer and more ignorant than me, Our

Lady would have chosen that person." Could this not be an example of *sola gratia*?

Once past all the shops, source of so much controversy and criticism, Lourdes offers a truly Gospel scene: a mixed group of people, just like the crowd which came to listen to Jesus, the sick in the front row and those blessés de la vie ("wounded by life") as Cardinal Honoré called them on the occasion of Pope John Paul II's pilgrimage to Tours in 1996.

The phenomenon of Lourdes started with Bernadette and not with the clerical authorities. The parish priest and bishop treated Bernadette with extreme caution and only after months of relentless investigation did they finally pronounce the authenticity of her testimony. The Church's pronouncement does not take away from the fact that Bernadette Soubirous was no more than a simple child who was called, as others too were called over the 2000 years of Christianity, to be instruments of spiritual renewal.

There is something profoundly evangelical about Lourdes, but deep-rooted difficulties still remain, such as the dogma of the Immaculate Conception, devotion to the saints and praying to Mary.

The Dombes Group

More recently, in the 1990s, a group of theologians, known as the Dombes Group, opened up the dialogue on Mary, and we are indebted to them for their work, which, though they did not realize this at the time, was to be of particular help to Lourdes. Founded in 1937 by Abbott Couturier, the group brought together key figures from the Catholic and Protestant Churches to study certain theological issues, such as the sacraments, the Church and its ministry. In an atmosphere of deep mutual trust they broached the subject of Mary. To their great surprise they discovered that their understanding of Mary bore no resemblance to the usual caricatures associated with her.

Supported by biblical and historical research they then decided to look at four areas which have traditionally been sources of conflict, including the Immaculate Conception and prayer to Our Lady. Although a consensus was not reached, the final text demonstrated their mutual openness to one another's views.

Lourdes as seen by Anglicans

The Anglican Church has various traditions, the oldest of which, (High Church), professes a deep veneration of Mary. When I was Bishop of Chartres, I regularly received a delegation from the Church of England from the diocese with which we were twinned. One of the first things they did was to go down to the crypt to venerate Mary, much to the astonishment of the Reformed Church pastor.

The first Anglican pilgrimage to Lourdes seems to have taken place in 1963, followed by an ecumenical pilgrimage of Catholic and Anglican nurses in 1971. Since then groups of Anglicans, Catholics and Presbyterians visit the shrine regularly. It often comes as a shock during the eucharistic procession for pilgrims who are unaccustomed to seeing women priests, to see them in procession in clerical attire. It is inevitable that ecumenism should meet with some lack of understanding

Lourdes as seen by Evangelical Christians

Mary's place in the Evangelical tradition is more limited. Its communities have only recently been established in Europe. Dialogue is just beginning, but what is far more important is the fact that their communities are expanding rapidly and globalisation necessitates that we work together.

Theologically speaking, a Marian spirituality is difficult for evangelicals, but they are renowned for their expression of faith through song and big gatherings and in this respect they may have much in common with Lourdes. They would certainly be welcome.

Lourdes as seen by the Orthodox

The veneration of Mary in the Orthodox tradition is very well known. However, there are other difficulties of which I will mention four.

– Orthodox Christianity has many places of pilgrimage and Marian shrines, for example the shrine of Potchaeu in Russia. But the tradition of Marian apparitions is less emphasized, than in the Latin world.

– The rosary in not known.

– The dogma of the Immaculate Conception, what it is about and how it came about, does not concern them.

– Concerning images of Mary, 19th century statues could not have been more different from the icon image, not only aesthetically but also in a theological, liturgical and spiritual sense. In eastern iconography, Mary is more often represented with the child.

Several avenues

So what chance does an Orthodox pilgrim have of feeling at

home in Lourdes. We have a record of an Orthodox pilgrimage in 1974.

Firstly, wherever he sees Mary, the Orthodox Christian is happy. Mary is all holy: *Panagia*. In essence the Roman Catholic dogma is saying the same, but in different words. One of their traditional icons represents the Virgin of compassion: pilgrims seek this same presence of Mary when they come to the Grotto, and she in her maternal way leads them to the grace of Christ.

Eastern Christianity is familiar with pilgrimages of all sizes and does not reject popular religious expression. They are not scandalised by people embracing the rock at the grotto, the blessing of medals and rosaries, or the drawing of water from the spring. The opposite is true for Christians from the Protestant tradition who would view these acts as a form of superstition.

Can Lourdes be an ecumenical meeting place?

Lourdes welcomes Christians of all traditions. Some aspects of Lourdes may irritate them, or at least, surprise them. In this respect they are not much different from Catholics themselves, many of whom are also surprised by what they find when they come to Lourdes.

All are able to nourish their faith. I have tried to point out similarities between the Christian traditions, but Lourdes also has a number of great biblical symbols which are the common heritage of all Christians, beyond their different traditions; for example, the wind preceding the first apparition, the rock, the water, and light, all symbols which flow through Scripture in both the New and Old Testament, and through the liturgy.

Ecumenical dialogue will not make progress unless each Christian tradition has the courage to be itself without being too superior or too modest. To appreciate each other's uniqueness we need to meet each other on home ground. Lourdes is a good example of openly Roman Catholic characteristics, without being superior or exclusive.

Its message to Christians of all other traditions is: "Please come. You will not be asked to do anything that may go against your convictions. Perhaps you will even find that our similarities are stronger than our differences."

Mgr Théas predicted that Lourdes would one day become a meeting point for ecumenism. He foresaw the construction of a huge ecumenical meeting hall, but because of the exceptionally high costs of the Pius X basilica, it has yet to be built. There is, however, a large marquee dedicated to ecumenism.

Rev. Jean Tartier

In 2000, talks began in Lourdes at which representatives from the Orthodox, Anglican and Reformed Churches took up the discussion of sensitive issues such as the Eucharist and Marian devotion. Each year too, when the plenary assembly of bishops meets, Christians of other traditions are represented by an important delegation from their Churches. Meeting in Lourdes does not seem to be a problem for them. A group of Reformed Church Christians attended the national catechesis convention held in Lourdes in 1979.

One of the most remarkable events has been the conference set up by the Rev. Jean Tartier, president of the French Protestant Federation, 10 years after the opening of the Pavillion for Christian Unity in Lourdes. On that occasion he declared that "the virginity of Mary is the sign, accepted by all, even Protestants, that the human person is incapable of giving birth to their own deliverance or to their own saviour. For this we need the miraculous freedom and the full gratuitousness of God."

After the death of Jesus, the soldiers did not tear and divide his tunic: Jesus gave us Mary to be Mother of the Church, how she rejoices at seeing her children gathered together here.

The Church and ecumenism

I would like to introduce myself. I am Arthur's mother. Arthur is 36 years old and he has come to Lourdes on a pilgrimage. He is in a wheelchair; he is unable to speak and needs help at all times. He was not born prematurely, but his brain failed to develop properly. What is Arthur's life like?

When Arthur smiles, all his family and friends smile. He loves music, company and laughter and gets quite excited and noisy. His joy is contagious, spilling over on to all of us. It is a grace. But Arthur's day to day life is also full of frustrations. He cannot react to his environment except by refusing to eat or drink or by hitting us when we need to cut his nails or wash his hair, or by crying for reasons we do not understand. Sometimes he sleeps the whole day. We worry about his welfare. Now an adult, he has lost the little bit of mobility for which we fought so long and hard. These have been traumatic times for us and it is often difficult to imagine what the future will hold. Who will look after him when we are too old?

Arthur has made an immense contribution to our lives and the lives of others. Throughout the years, he has been looked after by young people, some of whom have found their vocation in life through being with him. Now that my husband is retired he has taken up a new career working for charitable organisations for people with mental disabilities.

As for me, my ministry in life is intrinsically linked to my spiritual journey with Arthur; to my doubts, when faced with deep theological questions arising from our situation and also to the discovery, as parents of someone with a serious disability, of a deeper understanding of Christianity. I would like to share 3 reflections with you.

1 Mary

I am a Protestant. Mary has become very important to me. I identify with her. In her I find the model of faith of a mother whose son is suffering. When Arthur was about 15, I was struck by the image of Mary. It was Christmas time. We lived very near a Catholic convent and the nuns had invited all their neighbours to celebrate Midnight Mass with them. I went with Arthur in his wheelchair. It was the first time that I had been in a chapel with such a huge statue of the Blessed Virgin.

I was filled with the image of this statue and of Arthur as we sang Christmas carols. I began to regain my faith after battling inside for so many years. As I pushed Arthur home after Mass, a poem invaded my soul as if from nowhere:

Mary, my child is adorable.
Is yours adorable too?
He has little hands and feet,
curly hair and a sweet smile.

Mary, my child is suffering.
Is yours suffering too?
He is overcome with distress,
wounded by rejection
disfigured and worn,
silenced.

Mary, my heart is full.
Is yours full too?
It is filled with toil and suffering,
agony, ecstasy and victory,
sympathy, anger and compassion,
transfigured by the celebration of love...

Mary, my heart is rejoicing.
Is yours rejoicing too?

When I came to Lourdes in 1991, I relived this moment when I did the Way of the Cross and came to the place where Mary encountered Christ before his crucifixion. Mary became more and more real to me during my stay at Lourdes. A few years later, I searched for an image of the Pietà, of Mary cradling her dead son taken down from the cross. I understood that through the suffering of Mary's motherhood and the piercing of her heart, God had manifested his love. Mary has become a figure of contemplation for Protestants. This is very important because it helps us to grow together in deeper unity.

2 Christian Unity

I have always believed in ecumenism. Throughout my life I have sympathised with Christians from other traditions. My strongest ecumenical experiences have happened because of

Arthur. Thanks to him, I have come to accept differences and to build a spiritual unity.

Catholic organisations have been amongst the most welcoming towards Arthur. They have welcomed him into their communities and even taken him on holiday. The organisation known as the St Omer's Trust offered us student nurses and one of them, James, accompanied Arthur on a pilgrimage to Lourdes.

My strongest ecumenical experience was undoubtedly the Faith and Light Pilgrimage in 1991. The concluding ceremony was deeply moving. The scene where Mary Magdalene meets the risen Jesus in the garden was enacted by the Faith and Light Community. The part of Jesus was played by a man suffering from trisomy. Mary was played by a woman with severe learning difficulties. The symbolism was powerful when Jesus asked four of us representing different Churches, to love one another. I found myself being embraced by a cardinal, and by both Anglican and Catholic bishops. It was very moving for me to be a representative of the Protestant traditions and to be part of something much greater than myself. To honour the poor and weak was to break down the barriers of history and prejudice.

3 The bread of life that is broken

My final reflection is about what we receive in the Eucharist: the bread that is shared, which gives us faith, hope and life. As we break bread new possibilities are created.

Living with Arthur has enabled me to understand that Christianity is made up of values that are totally different from those in the world in which we live, which seeks success and wealth. The fruits of the Spirit of Jesus are love, joy, peace, patience, generosity, faithfulness, gentleness, self-control. These qualities emerge when people share their vulnerability, when the fragility of life is recognised, but also in the sacrament, when the bread which is broken touches those broken in body with love and care.

These are a few examples of the profound joy that parents who endure difficult trials may experience with the help of faith. It is a deep privilege to discover that there is hope, peace and joy in situations where the majority of people see only suffering and darkness. When you meet God in the person of Christ, questions give way to silence and sufferings fade away. As for me, I live the sacrament of the present moment in Arthur's smile.

Frances Young
Methodist minister
Experience given in Lourdes during the international
"Faith and Light" Pilgrimage, 2001.

CHAPTER FIVE

THE MISSION OF THE CHURCH
AND THE CALL FOR CONVERSION

Today we usually think of a convert as someone who has changed from one denomination or religion to another, or someone who has taken up a religion having had no previous religious conviction at all. This is not how it is in Scripture. When John the Baptist preached his message of conversion to all those who came to him to be baptised, he was preaching a message of repentance and forgiveness of sins. All those who heard him were Jews, so their faith was never in question. Instead, John was calling them to change their ways, and to respect the Law which commands us to worship the Lord our God and to do no harm to others. Jesus takes up the same message at the beginning of his public ministry. At that time there was no distinction between the Jews and Jesus' disciples.

"Repentance" or "conversion"?

The Gospel uses both these words. It is not possible to have one without the other. Through repentance we prepare our hearts and minds to receive something new. Without it the moment of conversion never comes. Someone who is immersed in sin is blinded by sin and is likely to refuse such a call, as it makes him feel uneasy. "Everybody who does wrong hates the light and avoids it to prevent his actions from being shown up" (John 3, 20). Most of all he is afraid of what he will see himself.

The Gospel shows us that self-importance, jealousy, power, reputation and wealth prevented the Jewish leaders from being open to the newness of Christ's message. They failed to hear John the Baptist's words: "Repent for the kingdom of heaven is close at hand" (Matthew 3, 2; 4, 17) or Jesus' words " Repent and believe the good news" (Mark 1, 15).

Pilate, on the other hand, represents the pagan world (with the exception of wonderful examples of faith like that of the Canaanite). Pilate is not required to follow Jewish law, but he yields to the same temptations as the Jewish leaders. He is concerned for his own career, knowing that the Jews will denounce him if he releases the man they say is calling himself the "King of the Jews", and so he condemns an innocent man.

The Gospel tells us that repentance is for everyone, Jews and pagans alike, if they truly desire the good news. "Whoever does the truth comes into the light" (John 3, 21). Pilate is sceptical about truth. He can merely ask "Truth? What is that?"

If we look at the lives of the saints, baptised as well as non-baptised, we often see that at one time they were leading a life that was far from the Gospel. God comes looking for them while they are still far away from him. Gradually they begin to experience remorsefulness for their sinful life and as they begin to turn away from their mistakes, God meets them at the moment of their conversion, turning their lives upside down. This is what happened to St Augustine and St Charles de Foucauld. The prodigal son, even though motivated by self-interest, understood that it was better for him to return to his father. As the Latin proverb goes: *errare, humanum est; perseverare, diabolicum* (to err is human, but to continue in error comes from the devil). The prodigal son realized that he had to turn away from the error of his ways.

A change of direction is obvious and necessary

Repentance, it seems, is in keeping with our times, some might say excessively so. It is easier to criticise the past and the errors of those no longer with us than it is to change ourselves. We try to put the blame on our predecessors. This is unjust and dishonest, because times are different now to what they were. We cannot reconstruct the climate of the past. It is better to ask ourselves what we can do today than to think about what should have been done in the past.

When Pope John Paul II invited the whole Catholic Church to repentance during the jubilee year 2000, it was in order to look forwards, not backwards; to set out on the path of evangelisation at the beginning of the 3rd millennium. Repentance means turning back to the One who sees into the depths of our hearts. It is not about asking God to forgive those who have already left this world.

Neither they, nor we, are able to wipe the slate clean. If we do not hand over the past to God, there is a great danger that we end up feeling guilty, having a low opinion of ourselves, or feel self-justified. Repentance is a delicate matter.

However, it is better to regret the past than to refuse to look at it at all. This balance is not easy, as we do not always see things clearly. Where do the real weaknesses lie and what should we do about them? Our civilisation knows that it cannot continue indefinitely on its present path. Over-emphasizing personal freedom leaves people without boundaries; it increases inequalities and breaks down community spirit. Exploiting natural resources without restraint increases fear about the future of our planet. Seeking cheap solutions rather than listening to reason, creates a type of mass sensationalism which is easy to manipulate. We are bombarded by so much information, so much noise and so many images that we are not able to think or reflect sufficiently. The list of wrongs generated by a permissive society and culture seems endless. However, having said that, the wrongs committed by 20th century dictators are worse still.

Should we be the ones to make amends for wrongs committed in the past? Maybe the excesses we so deplore were inevitable because they were "sins of youth". Despite the fact that the word "change" gets misused and tarnished during election campaigns, we can easily argue that a change of direction is necessary. It is our modern, secular, understanding of "conversion".

Turning to God

Our religious understanding of conversion, turning back to God, is not considered so modern! Nowadays people seem to reject any idea connected with revelation. They do not wish to conform to a law they haven't written, let alone one they cannot change every few years.

In 1858 the religious scene in Lourdes was very different

70

from today. Even so, amongst leading members of society reason was already taking the place of faith.

Even a well-known Catholic like Councillor Massy thought that a phenomenon like Lourdes with its apparitions and cures put religion in a bad light. "Pilgrimages are no longer in fashion," said a certain Mr Thiers. We must maintain the bourgeois order both within religion and as a result of religion.

Once again, it is the saints who break through these narrow-minded beliefs. 19th century France may be the century of conformism, but it is also the century of Ozanam, the Curé d'Ars, and Thérèse of Lisieux. It is the era of African and Asian missionaries who left without hope of returning, and many of whom became martyrs. It is also the century of Bernadette, who speaks of "another world" shining through her transfigured face.

The most difficult conversion of all is to move away from self, to cease thinking of oneself as the centre of the universe, as the beginning and end of one's own existence, the supreme judge of what is good and true. When an individual or group behaves in this egocentric way they mistake their shadows for light and are imprisoned by them. We have arrived at the very root of sin.

Lourdes, a place of conversion

The Church's mission is to show that self-centredness leads nowhere and to point to another way, by announcing the Gospel, by the witness of saints, of communities and the faithful, and by works of art inspired by the divine. Lourdes is an invitation to conversion, for several reasons.

The fact that so many people come to Lourdes shows that the search for the meaning of life is not out of date. It can be a new discovery just to see others praying in large numbers, and to realize that it is not only Muslims with their own special gestures, who do this. Prayer or just silence opens the door to a world previously unknown and to a deep sense of peace.

To see all the sick, aged and disabled is a moving experience. Normally they are hidden, but at Lourdes they are in the front line, surrounded by their smiling helpers. Seeing them, we find ourselves questioning what is of real value in this life.

Like her contemporaries, many are intrigued by Bernadette's personality. This saint was a wonderful mixture of realism, humour, courage and faith. Nothing could distract her from her path to sanctity once she had entered the convent at Nevers.

At Lourdes, you do not have to call Mary by her title "The Immaculate Conception" to be able to confide in her. She welcomes all who come to her at the Grotto. No one misbehaves in the presence of their heavenly mother. The atmosphere of the Grotto is maternal.

At Lourdes, many paths lead to conversion and many ways can be found to express the desire for conversion: drinking from the fountains; (one thinks of the living water that Jesus speaks of to the Samaritan women); washing one's face at the fountains; entering the baths; the Way of the Cross; the Grotto which no one passes through without praying to leave it renewed. As we read in the guidebooks, Lourdes is not a place for long speeches. For many pilgrims, the high point is the sacrament of reconciliation, which is widely available at Lourdes.

The communion of saints

For those who have strayed far from God the experience of Lourdes may not come naturally at first, but no one is left on their own. Christ the Good Shepherd goes to look for the lost sheep. The Blessed Virgin is the "refuge of sinners". I find myself surrounded by brothers and sisters like me: they pray and offer up their sufferings and go out to serve others. They carry me along.

Bernadette herself leads the way in praying for the conversion of sinners. Between the 8th and 12th apparition (24th February – 1st March, there was no apparition on the 26th), Bernadette behaved very strangely. She crawled and prostrated herself on the ground; she ate grass; she tried in vain to drink some water from a tiny puddle she had dug with her hands, and her face, which was normally radiant, was smeared with mud. Only after four attempts did she manage to swallow some water from the spring which no one knew existed.

Taking her for an idiot, Bernadette was brought before the imperial procurator on 25th February. She did not waste time trying to explain her actions. The Blessed Virgin's message consisted of just a few words: "Penance, penance. Pray for sinners." That was all she was doing, Bernadette would say, as well as praying for herself and others. Throughout her life Bernadette offered her humiliations and sufferings for sinners. At Lourdes, we are not alone; we have Our Lady and St Bernadette. We participate in the communion of saints.

Isaiah speaks of the Servant of God: "Ours were the sufferings he was bearing, ours the sorrows he was carrying" (Isaiah 53, 4). Christ is the Suffering Servant. Bernadette imitated her Lord and we are invited to do the same, in spite of whether prayer and penance happen to be in keeping with the times or not. Perhaps we are simply not reading the signs of the times correctly.

From that day, the trickle of muddy water became a clear running stream, flowing into fountains and troughs on the way to the pool. This is the water that pilgrims take home with them and give to others; the water which Christians from every continent come to receive. Bernadette said that this water had no value without faith and prayer. With faith and prayer it is a marvellous symbol; the painful tears of penance are transformed into tears of joy, and this joy irrigates the body of the Church throughout the world.

PERSONAL EXPERIENCE

Conversion and reconciliation

One day I met a priest (wearing clothes which seemed more suited to a woman, made of wool and in the middle of August!) He was a Dominican. (I had never heard of them!) He came over to me, and started talking to me and I felt embarrassed because of his strange attire. He came up to my motorbike, I revved it up noisily and offered him a ride. Judging by his age, he must have been about 70, so I thought he would say no. To my great surprise he said yes. When we had finished our deliberately bumpy ride which I had done to try and scare him, I thought he was going to give me the telling off I deserved but he told me how much he had enjoyed it and did I want to receive forgiveness from Jesus. I asked him what that was. He told me that it would "do me good", then he took my hand and started praying, his eyes closed and his lips moving silently. I told him I was a non-believer. He looked at me in a friendly way, placed my hand on my heart, saying: "Jesus knows what is in your heart. He loves you, and forgives you." At that moment I said to myself: "I must be mad not to try something that might do me good."

That was my first experience of forgiveness. I didn't understand anything, but it certainly hadn't done me any harm. I went back to Fr Thomas-Philippe* many times and on each occasion he offered me the forgiveness of Jesus as if for the first time. I didn't go for that reason, although I never once felt that I didn't need it. I carried on receiving the forgiveness of Jesus for several months. Fr Thomas-Philippe recited the prayers slowly so that I could join in and they began to penetrate me. Each time I received the sacrament was like a delicate murmuring to my sinful heart and soul which was little by little becoming tame. What drew me each time was discovering the gentleness of God, the Big Boss, through the actions of his servant. Never once did I feel my confidence would be betrayed. By his invitation, each time given as a free and unique gift, I fell in love with the mystery of the Church. That is how I came to want to know more about the family of the Church, about the Big Boss's gang.

I thank the priests who are not afraid to offer Jesus' forgiveness, especially to those who haven't asked for it. People full of love usually offer a glass of water, a coffee or some biscuits... I thank the Big Boss for calling people to the priesthood. When they prostrate themselves on the ground at the moment of their ordination, it is in order to be covered with all the graces they will need throughout their priesthood through each sacrament. When they do this act, they never exhaust the graces they are given, and therefore one should never be afraid of going to tell a priest all the burdens in life.

* Co-founder of l'Arche together with Jean Vanier

Each time we receive the sacrament of reconciliation it is like a drop that sweetly transfuses our future to the point of becoming the flavour and taste of living a better life. For me, each confession is a chance to place my heart in the wound of the pierced Christ. By giving me forgiveness, it is as though he has taken me by the hand to forgive my father, who had led me along paths of hatred. I always used to say I wanted to kill him. Whenever I met elderly people who were at peace with their painful past, it used to annoy me. At the same time I admired them, although it annoyed me that they didn't feel any hatred. Without knowing it, they were preparing me for the unknown path of forgiveness and to help me let go of my memories. Forgiveness is not magic, neither for the person granting it nor for the person who does not know that he going to be forgiven. It does not dissolve like instant coffee. I wanted to be the conqueror when I forgave, forcing my father back to the past. Suddenly the moment came when he could no longer forgive himself. Then I understood that the way God forgives was not by sending my father back to the past, but by making him part of each new moment that I now had.

Sometimes we human beings imprison others with our forgiveness, but the forgiveness of God can only liberate. Just as we remember the date of our birthday we can sometimes also remember the dates of our sufferings. Forgiveness is about letting go of our injuries in order to give ourselves the right to exist, not to commit the same crimes, to start new, with the help of the Big Boss and his gang of saints known and unknown.

The father of the prodigal son loved his son throughout all his wrongdoing. He loved him even when he left, we do not know for how long, 3 months, 3 years, 30 years .... He waited for him each day. The son didn't even have a chance to explain. Because of his father's love he didn't even need to explain. God never demands an explanation.

Neither did Bernadette give any explanation: "I have been entrusted to give you this message not to make you believe it." At Lourdes, the Blessed Virgin sent Bernadette in the direction of the priests: "Go and tell the priests," and in the direction of sinners: "Penance, penance, pray for sinners".

For 150 years priests have been present at Lourdes to free people's hearts. Many people arrive overburdened yet leave released from their bonds, daring to become new people. Thanks to Mary and Bernadette, Lourdes is the place where the Father awaits his prodigal child.

Tim Guénard

CHAPTER SIX

THE MISSION OF THE CHURCH
AND SICK PEOPLE

From the moment Our Lady revealed her name as the Immaculate Conception, the sick have had a special place at Lourdes. When people think of Lourdes they think of miracles. Yet miracles are rare in Lourdes. Although they are important, and I will speak about them later, the presence of the sick is even more significant.

By welcoming the sick, Lourdes is a living example of Jesus' words "I was sick and you visited me" or more precisely "you welcomed me".

Illness and healing in Scripture

It is often said that Jesus was surrounded by the poor. This is only partly true. Zaccheus, Lazarus and his sisters, and the "disciple Jesus loved" were not poor. What is truer is that Jesus was constantly surrounded by the sick. The evangelists had sufficient medical knowledge at the time of writing, to know how to distinguish between those who were sick in body and those who were sick in spirit. A physical ailment did not mean there was a devil to be cast out. The sick are, therefore, much more than a "symbolic presence" in the Gospel. Their physical healing is real and important, not just an "outward sign" of the deeper healing within.

The sick who came to Jesus were truly seeking a cure because medicine at that time was often ineffective. Even so, there is great respect towards the medical profession in both the Jewish and Christian traditions. Just as the artist and the farmer reflect the wisdom of God, so too does the doctor. The book of Ecclesiastes (38) tells us the right attitude to have towards doctors and the right attitude that doctors should have towards God their creator, in whose work they are co-operating.

Even a little satire can be used. In the cure of the woman with a haemorrhage, St Mark's account is the most ironic: "After long and painful treatment under various doctors, she had spent all she had without being any the better for it" (Mark 5, 26). Her experience reminds us of certain quack doctors today. However, St Paul does not hesitate to address his disciple Luke as "My dear doctor".

When faced with suffering and illness Christians strive to find a meaningful balance between the spiritual and human aspect. They do not rush to give illness a purely spiritual interpretation, thereby ignoring the possibilities which the Creator himself gives us of finding a cure.

Jesus gives us the example of the Good Samaritan to teach us about love for our neighbour. The Samaritan actively looks after the wounded man by the side of the road, not simply sparing him a pious thought.

Jesus never turned the sick away. When he sends his disciples out in pairs he entrusts the sick to them as well as those possessed by unclean spirits. "So they set off to proclaim repentance; and they cast out many devils and anointed many sick people with oil and cured them" (Mark 6, 12).

Helping the sick down the centuries

Amongst the humanitarian works of the Church, care of the sick has always been as important an undertaking as helping the poor and providing education. St Basil, one of the great bishops of the 4th century and a doctor of the Holy Spirit, also founded hospitals. Similarly, when the great Cathedral of Notre Dame de Paris was being built, Bishop Maurice de Sully divided the funds equally between the Cathedral and the restoration of the 'Hotel-Dieu' alongside it. During the Crusades, a knight's first duty was to take care of the sick.

The Hospice at Baune, now a museum, is well-known for its annual sale of prestigious wine. However, the beauty of the building, both inside and out, still reflects the respect and love we should show our suffering brothers and sisters who are the suffering members of Christ's body.

Countless numbers of religious congregations have been founded in service of the sick. Amongst the most famous of founders is a Portuguese saint, St John of God (1495 – 1550) and an Italian saint, Camillo de Lellis (1550-1614). They are the patron saints of the world of health but only part of a great cohort of others.

Care of the poor, and education, especially that of girls, was often added to care of the sick. For example, all three were present in the work of the Sisters of Charity and Christian Instruction, the "Sisters of Nevers". They welcomed Bernadette, a local girl, and gave her instruction and it was with them that later she was to discover her vocation to serve Christ in her sick brothers and sisters, especially the most wretched and repulsive.

John Paul II addresses the sick

It is important to remember that the Christian view of pain and suffering is very much rooted in reality. In front of someone who is suffering, it is not possible to simply say in faith "Be brave; it will go away; it's only an illusion."

Let us listen to the words of Pope John Paul II, an expert in this field. It is he who introduced the World Day for the Sick, fixing it on the feast of Our Lady of Lourdes. It is he who founded the Pontifical Council for the World of Health. Above all, it is he who on several occasions, experienced physical suffering that brought him close to death's door. On the 15th August 1983, he gave the following address in Lourdes to all the sick gathered there; it was just two years after the assassination attempt which nearly cost him his life, and the consequences of which took him back many times to the Gemelli Hospital for further treatment.

"Suffering is always a reality, a reality with a thousand different faces. Before every suffering, the healthy have but one duty: respect, even silence... Neither fair nor unfair, the suffering remains, despite partial explanations which are difficult to comprehend and even harder to accept, even for those who have faith. Faith does not take away the pain. It links it invisibly to the suffering of Christ the Redeemer."

The Pope goes on to say that he would like to leave them with "three small candles" to mark the three stages of their journey in faith.

"Whatever your suffering, all that matters is that you are able to perceive it clearly, without undervaluing it or exaggerating it, and that you are able to experience the swirl of emotions of your human sensitivity: failure, a feeling of uselessness, etc.

"Then we must progress along the way of acceptance, believing in the promise that God not only can, but desires to, draw out good from every difficulty.

"And finally, the most beautiful gesture of all: our offering. The gift of our offering out of love for God and for others can take us to a high level of Christian virtue, namely losing ourselves in the love of Christ and the Most Holy Trinity for the sake of humanity.

"These three stages, lived out by the person who is suffering, according to his own individual rhythm and grace, lead him to an unimagined interior liberation."

The Pope concludes by lighting a fourth candle, that of the Church:

"Dearest suffering brothers and sisters, may you leave Lourdes fortified and renewed by your 'special mission'. You are precious in God's sight as those who co-operate with Christ in the Redemption in the reality of time and space."

His words had even greater resonance because of his personal experience; words full of realism and respect towards each person's own individual path; words full of spiritual ambition. The Pope continues his reflections in his encyclical *Salvifici doloris* (1984).

The mission of Lourdes

How can Lourdes help the Church in her responsibility to serve and be a witness in the world of health? The very first way to serve is outlined by the Pope just before the address we have just quoted: "Is not Lourdes the place par excellence where the sick are truly at home, in the same way as those who are healthy." The key word here surely is "in the same way"? At Lourdes every effort is made to ensure that everyone can participate in each other's events – for example the eucharistic and torchlight processions. Those responsible for organising the pilgrimages give special value to these moments lived in common and rightly so.

As they battle with their illness, the first who strive to accept their suffering are the sick themselves, and it is not easy. Acceptance is the second stage of that inner liberation to which the Pope refers. It is not only difficult for those who are sick but also for those who are well; they cannot ignore the fact that illness can occur at any time. They feel afraid of the unknown, wondering how they will bear it if it comes. At Lourdes, for the healthy as well as the sick, fear is taken away once and for all by the atmosphere of peace and joy. There is no room for any pseudo-mystical emotion.

This atmosphere is especially important for young people and children. Often they have not encountered illness; their grandparents, for the most part, are in good health. Medical care is more advanced and the quality of life for those in their seventies is much improved. Nevertheless, illness and death can never be excluded from the human condition, even though society only seems interested in them from a technical or statistical point of view, not taking into account the full human and spiritual dimensions involved. Lourdes can be an opportunity to reflect on these questions from a Christian perspective. Suffering and death are not the ultimate evil. Hope is possible, and brings light to the present.

The role of health

Keeping the words of John Paul II in mind, we come to the third stage of interior liberation to which he refers: that of offering up our suffering in communion with Christ the Saviour. There is nothing morbid and gloomy about Christian spirituality: the Gospel never shows us a Jesus who is ill, "Yet ours were the sufferings he bore and the sorrows he carried," according to the Prophet Isaiah, speaking of the suffering servant (Isaiah 53, 4). Jesus took our sufferings upon himself so as to heal them, and his miracles are a testimony to this: "He drove out many spirits with a command and cured all who were sick. This was to fulfil what was spoken by the prophet Isaiah" (Matthew 8, 17). Jesus bore our pain: we must not forget that we have been saved by his passion and that the same thing happens in his disciples.

"It makes me happy to be suffering for you now, and in my own body to make up all the hardships that still have to be undergone by Christ for the sake of his body, the Church." (Colossians 1, 24) Paul is not speaking of physical trials only, but of his "daily obsession, his concern for all the churches." St Paul always mentions the physical dimension. He is not a spiritual being without a body (2 Corinthians 11, 23-28).

A Christian is asked to go beyond even acceptance and detachment. Suffering, though worthless in itself, can become an offering for the healing of the world. This was Bernadette's own experience during the apparitions when the Blessed Virgin asked her to drink muddy water from the spring which did not yet exist at the Grotto: Bernadette obeyed "for the sake of sinners". As the cures multiplied at Lourdes, she herself had very poor health. Often ill, she came close to death several times. Yet she is the saint we continue to love, long after the names of those who have been miraculously cured have been forgotten. Whether we like it or not, there is no Christianity without the cross.

The Sacraments of the sick and the eucharistic procession

It is fitting that we refer to the sacraments of the sick in the plural, because it does not solely refer to the anointing of the sick but to two other sacraments as well which have a special significance for the sick: firstly, the sacrament of reconciliation, because in facing death we are also forced to face the life we have lived, and secondly the Eucharist, which is communion with the passion of Christ, "the bread which gives strength" and the guarantee of eternal life. However, let us pause for a moment at the anointing of the sick.

Lourdes has played a definitive role in the anointing of the sick. Mgr Théas received this sacrament when he suffered a heart attack in 1952. He preferred to call it "the last rites", the term that is officially used today. He wrote to his diocese in 1953: "Our loving mother, the Church, is close to those who are dying. But she wishes to be present before then, whilst they are ill. She wishes to heal and comfort them in her own special way, with the oil of the sick, entrusted to her by Christ." This orientation is validated by the Second Vatican Council in its Constitution on the Liturgy (no 72): "The sacrament may be given once a person's life is in danger or they are no longer able to survive on their own."

Through its witness, Lourdes helps us to understand that the anointing of the sick is not reserved only for those who are dying but is for all those who endure serious illness and disability. To those in their final agony the Church gives communion "by viaticum" for their passage from this life.

It is wrong to think that our understanding of the sacrament of the sick is always totally in line with the Church, but thanks to Lourdes, progress has been achieved and will continue to be achieved. For example, an incorrect tendency has arisen, which treats the anointing of the sick as a type of blessing for the elderly, which can be received every year, even in cases where there are no specific health problems. Lourdes needs to be vigilant in this respect.

The anointing must only be offered to those whose lives are gravely affected by illness or who are no longer able to survive on their own. By making the anointing of the sick one of the seven sacraments, the Church demonstrates the special importance given by Christ to the sick: illness is a state of life that demands a special grace.

Lourdes has also brought about another change. No longer restricted to the bedside of the dying, Vatican II has given the sacrament a liturgical expression and ecclesial dimension. It is no longer "administered" but celebrated, either collectively, as in places like Lourdes, or individually. Someone who is gravely ill is an active member of the communion of saints and a community may gather together to pray with them.

At Lourdes, this reality is expressed every day in the Eucharistic procession. The original purpose of this procession was to transfer the Blessed Sacrament to the place where the sick were to be blessed. Nowadays the sick take part in the procession in the same way as pilgrims who are well. Together they make up the Church as she journeys in pilgrimage towards Christ who has died and is risen. More than anyone else, the sick are invited to believe and hope in the Resurrection. To whoever receives the anointing of the sick, St James writes, "The Lord will raise him up again." He uses the language of the Resurrection.

And what about miracles?

And on that note I will reflect for a moment on miracles. I will not speak about the actual conditions required in order that a cure may be considered a miracle: that is a separate matter. Rather I will ask the question: What is the Christian meaning of a miracle? When Jesus cured a sick person or raised someone from the dead, he anticipated the Resurrection. Particularly symbolic is the cure of the leper; his decaying skin was healed, like the flowering of a new youth.

In the same way, miraculous cures today are a sign of hope. They anticipate, at least for a time, (for even someone who is cured must die) the Resurrection of the body that we look forward to in the Creed. We must not dismiss miracles as though they come from a pagan mentality, unworthy of the faith we place in Christ our only Saviour.

PERSONAL EXPERIENCE

The Sick

At 10 o'clock in the evening, on Sunday 14 October 2001, after four years of battling against cancer, Viviane "left for the next life". For the last few months we had cared for her at home in Paris with the help of the François-Xavier Bagnoux Centre. There were about ten of us at her bedside, including seven of our children or their spouses. Our grandchildren had come to see their grandmother that afternoon for the last time. Our daughter Gaëlle held one of her mother's hands and I held the other: life continued to pass through our joined hands right to the end. We kept silent watch as her breathing became less and less frequent. After a pause of more than five minutes I turned to my children, with the words "It's over now". The nurse and night watch entered the room just at that moment.

There are no words to express what it is like when someone you have loved for forty years is gone forever. I made a suggestion that we pray together next to Viviane's body, using the evening readings of October 14th from the monthly Magnificat magazine. As I read them I was profoundly moved; they seemed to have been specially chosen for that moment.

"Remember the Gospel that I carry, 'Jesus Christ risen from the dead'. If we have died with him, then we shall live with him. He is our salvation and eternal glory" (2 Timothy 2: 8, 13).

"The servants of the Lord will see him face to face and his name will be written on their foreheads. Night will be abolished; they will no longer need lamp or sunlight, because the Lord God will be shining on them. They will reign for ever and ever" (Apocalypse 22: 4,5).

"Lord our God, you let us hear your love on the morning of the Resurrection. When it is our turn to die, may your breath of life guide us to your presence. Through our Lord, Jesus Christ Amen."

"Into your hands O Lord I commend my spirit. Let your face shine upon your servant. Glory be to the Father, and to the Son, and to the Holy Spirit. Into your hands O Lord I commend my spirit."

Two contrasting thoughts came to my mind. Immense sadness at the thought of never being able to see again someone who was everything to me, and at the same time the relief of knowing that she was no longer suffering but in peace. A profound conviction invaded my soul, the certainty that Viviane had gone straight to the God in whom she had placed her trust and faith, that faith she had not let go of throughout the duration of her illness.

In 1995 I myself had been operated on for cancer, but in a much less advanced stage than Viviane's. On that occasion, we participated for the first time in the "Lourdes Cancer-Espérance" (L.C.E.) Pilgrimage, (Lourdes Cancer Hope). We were overwhelmed by the warmth and solidarity which animated thousands of pilgrims affected by cancer in body and heart. From that moment the Virgin of Massabielle had a special place in our lives. We returned to Lourdes with L.C.E. for the next two years. In 1998, we accompanied our friends there in spirit only as Viviane was by then in hospital, after intense chemotherapy treatment following her second operation. The next three years we lived exceptional moments at Lourdes with L.C.E., but Viviane's health was deteriorating. In 1999 and in 2000 she was in a wheelchair. In 2001, she was carried on a stretcher to receive the anointing of the sick at the Church of St Bernadette. She had deeply longed for this pilgrimage and it was with great peace that just four weeks later she went to meet the Lord.

It is thanks to L.C.E. that we met Anne-Marie Jaouen at the beginning of 2000, and very quickly a true friendship was formed between herself and Viviane. Anne-Marie lived in Brest where she helped to spread and develop L.C.E. in the Finistère region.

At the beginning of October 2000, I realized that I could no longer leave Viviane alone because of her loss of balance as the cancer spread to the brain. The day I realised this, Anne-Marie called me from Brest for news. When I told her that things were not good, that I couldn't leave her on her own and didn't know what to do with regard to my work, Anne-Marie replied: "Yann, if you will allow me, I am coming straight away." Two days later she arrived with her small suitcase and she stayed with us totally voluntarily for the next year, looking after Viviane like a daughter, until her death on October 14th 2001.

There are other miracles in Lourdes apart from physical ones. It was Anne-Marie who had introduced us to the habit of reading the reading of the day together from the magazine Magnificat. That is why it was so natural for me to read that day's readings on the night that Viviane died. The texts that I have quoted came up again several times throughout the course of the next year. The first time on 2 December, feast of St Viviane! And twice on days when I had felt a particular presence of the Communion of Saints

A year later, on the 2002 pilgrimage, which I attended for the first time without Viviane, when Fr Joulia approached me and asked me if I would take over from him as pilgrimage director, I knew I could not refuse his request. Since then I have received such comfort and graces in preparing our annual pilgrimages with the rest of the team. The sight of the green and white scarves carried in Lourdes by 500 pilgrims of L.C.E. coming from all over France, Belgium and Monaco, is a source of deep joy for me, and of faith that this life will never end and that we shall one day meet our loved ones again.

Yann Pivet
Pilgrimage director of L.C.E.
(Lourdes Cancer Espérance)

CHAPTER SEVEN

THE MISSION OF THE CHURCH AND PEOPLE WITH DISABILITIES

At Lourdes, we often refer to the sick and disabled together, but we need to be aware of the subtle differences between them. For example, we can fall ill and know we are going to get better or we can fall ill and know we are not going to get better; we may be blind from birth or we may become blind, gradually or suddenly in an accident. Each case is entirely different, lived in a unique and personal way.

Everybody has an idea of what illness is, even if their experience has not been life-threatening, but not everyone understands what disability is. Broadly speaking, it is the absence or deficiency of a physical or mental capacity, whether from birth or otherwise.

The Gospel recounts many episodes which are about the disabled - the deaf and dumb, blind and paralysed. There are not so many episodes concerning those with a mental disability.

Much less was known then about mental illness and its causes. It was usually associated with unclean spirits. Jesus reached out to the man down among the tombs that "howled and gashed himself with stones day and night" (Mark 5, 5). Jesus healed him and restored him to sanity. Whatever the causes of mental disability, we, like Jesus, must always protect its victims from being alienated.

Different types of disability

The disabled have never been excluded from Lourdes. The first seven miracle cures were directly related to physical disabilities: paralysis, semi-paralysis, blindness and so on.

Nevertheless, the first buildings at Lourdes were not properly accessible to those who were not fully mobile. To try and rectify this, a ramp was added in front of the Rosary Basilica, but the slope was too steep and it had to be abandoned. A completely new ramp with proper accessibility was completed in 2001.

The first real change in mentality came about in 1958 with the construction of the St Pius X underground basilica. Steps disappeared altogether and access in all directions was by gently sloping ramps.

Over the years pilgrimages have been organised aimed at specific disabilities. The first pilgrimage for the blind took place in July 1946. Today, the blind can use a special tactile plan which enables them to discover through touch the layout of the shrine, the shape of the grotto and the architecture of the monuments.

A pilgrimage for those suffering from polio proved to be much more difficult. It was hoped that something could be done in time for the centenary in 1958, but the French railway company SNCF was unable to guarantee the safety of the respiratory equipment and the project could not go ahead. It was not until 1963 that Doctor Cattenoz managed to bring 500 polio victims to Lourdes. By 1968 the number had grown to 3000.

For those involved in sport, able-bodied and disabled athletes share their pilgrimage together.

There is still much to do, particularly for the deaf and hearing-impaired.

We who are able-bodied do not know what it is like to live with a permanent disability or what effect this has upon their spirit. The awareness we seek in Lourdes must be the same for all Christian communities.

At Lourdes we welcome a great number of disabled people, more so because today people are living longer. We have time to listen to them and find ways of helping them integrate into society. Our responsibility at Lourdes is to be a social model for the rest of the Church on how to welcome the disabled.

An able-bodied person must learn to discern when it is appropriate for them to use all their God-given strength and abilities to help someone less able than themselves without feeling guilty, or when, out of respect, it is inappropriate to do so. In other words, he or she must learn how to serve. Serving is reciprocal. The disabled teach us to appreciate the gift of health, but also to admire the ways in which human beings are able to adapt when faced with a disability.

Mental illness generates fear

Physical disability has always been present at the heart of Lourdes. This it is not the case with mental disability. The field of mental illness is huge and complex and the subject of much controversy.

Lourdes has remained cautious in such matters, just as it was at the time of the apparitions. If we seek to explain away the mystery of the human spirit with the same reason and scientific precision that we apply to the physical world, how then can we explain the divine?

At the time of the apparitions, the chief of police, Monsieur Massy, longed to put a stop to the stream of people coming to the grotto by declaring Bernadette mad and having her taken away. He had already failed to have her taken away for being a trouble-maker. So, to achieve his aim, he set up a commission of three doctors who interrogated Bernadette on 27 March 1858. Despite not wishing to disappoint the chief of police, they could find no reason why, on health grounds, she should not remain free. Of course, advanced hallucinations were a possibility, but there was no real proof.

These three doctors followed their professional consciences with integrity. But the actions of the chief inspector, who was a Catholic, illustrated the climate of the time: everything had to be explained by nervous disorders or the processes of hallucination.

In this context we can appreciate why the chaplains and doctors connected with the shrine have always preferred to deal with illnesses and disabilities of the body: they did not wish to expose themselves to professional criticism by declaring a mentally ill person healed, when that person may have simply undergone a religious experience. Wishing to avoid the traps of this medical minefield so full of uncertainty, they naturally preferred to ignore this area.

Until recently, pilgrimage organisers were advised not to bring the mentally ill and in the event of declaring a cure, all suspicion of mental problems needs to have been ruled out. I am not sure whether this still holds true today.

A variety of initiatives

Throughout history, many religious communities, both men's and women's, have dedicated themselves to the care of people suffering from mental disability or illness, the most well-known being the Brothers of St John of God, founded in 1525.

The first raising of awareness towards the disabled at Lourdes, whether physical, mental or both, came from the Anglo-Saxon countries. The first HCPT pilgrimage (Handicapped Children's Pilgrimage Trust) took place in 1956. For the first few years, the children who came suffered from more minor disabilities, but in time, the boundaries receded and the organisation was able to cater for all types of disability. In the most difficult cases, the parents come too in order to help interpret their children's gestures and express their needs.

HCPT pilgrimages take place each year at Easter and are one of the "highlights" of the season. You cannot fail to notice them, the children are all dressed alike with joy radiating from their faces: the joy of being together beneath Mary's maternal gaze, living together as brothers and sisters in Gospel simplicity, able to mix freely with ordinary pilgrims, knowing that they, the smallest and the least, are the ones to whom the secrets of the kingdom of heaven have been revealed.

Of all the pilgrimages that take place during the year, this is one of the closest to the message of Lourdes. Bernadette herself would have identified with these children, as having the same spirit as her. She would have had no problem communicating with them.

Coming to Lourdes at Easter, which is traditionally when Lourdes begins its new year, the HCPT pilgrimage truly gives Lourdes an injection of youthfulness.

In 1963, Marie-Hélène Matthieu set up the French Christian Bureau for the Disabled to provide mutual support for families with disabled members. The following year, 1964, Jean Vanier founded L'Arche. His idea of communities of able-bodied and disabled people living together was revolutionary.

A turning point for Lourdes was the Faith and Light pilgrimage in 1971 inspired by Jean Vanier, who realized that the mentally disabled needed a special place in Lourdes. Thus the Faith and Light Movement was born which gathers at Lourdes every 10 years, most recently in 2001. Many disabled people also returned in 2004 to hear Jean Vanier meditate aloud the luminous mysteries of the rosary in the presence of John Paul II.

Since 1972 there has been a permanent centre for disabled people, including their families and friends. It serves two purposes: to support them during their few days' pilgrimage and to support them long-term with information about communities and movements who can help them become less marginalized back at home. This permanent centre forms part of the Welcome Centres within the shrine itself.

From Paul VI to John Paul II

In 1971 the Faith and Light pilgrimage received a special message from Pope Paul VI. It touches on key themes later developed by John Paul II.

Dearest friends, at times your spirit is crushed and your hearts saddened with the pain of not being able to study, work and build relationships as easily as others... All people have weaknesses and disabilities, some secret or hidden. Be assured, you have a special place in society. In the midst of people intoxicated with output and efficiency, you are there with your simplicity and your joy, with your gaze which seeks out unconditional love, a love given freely; with your wonderful capacity to understand the expressions of such a love and your delicate responses. In the Church too, which is above all a House of Prayer, you have an even more special role: to understand the innermost secrets of God, and to entreat him, for Christ listens to you in a privileged way.

The Pope goes on to address parents, professionals, political leaders and pastors.

And you, dear parents... we are filled with awe as we contemplate the heroic love that you have for your child. Yes, look upon your child with the same tenderness as God...

Friends and neighbours do not hesitate to visit and welcome these brothers and sisters. Build friendships with the greatest simplicity.

(To professionals) *May your witness shatter the materialism of an indifferent society which no longer properly respects life, which all too willingly closes its eyes to anything that is not comfortable, powerful and efficient...*

Leaders, make your plans without excluding those who have been disowned by their country. This is the true test of human solidarity that you are keen to demonstrate in your policies.

And you, shepherds and pastors of the Church, may you understand how to let the weak and the helpless know how special they are, in the same way that Jesus did.

During John Paul II's Pontificate the number of gatherings for the disabled and sick greatly increased. He believed in them:

"We need to discover their spiritual openness and foster their Christian formation." (Pilgrimage of Faith and Light, Lourdes 1991). It is not only charity that demands this attitude, but our very humanity, from which our dignity comes.

"The quality of a society or civilisation can be measured by its respect for its members who are the least. A society which is technically perfect, which only welcomes members who are fully productive, is not worthy of being called human; it is perverted by a form of discrimination as condemning as racial discrimination. The disabled person is one of us, participating in our own humanity. To recognise and promote their dignity and their rights is to recognise our own dignity and rights." (Québec, September 1984.)

(To the disabled) *"Perhaps you are sometimes afraid of being a burden here on earth. Perhaps you have been made to feel this way. If this is so, I ask your forgiveness on behalf of humanity. It is true that you need us, our help and our care, our hands and our hearts. But we most certainly need you."* (Vienna, 12 September 1983)

An urgent mission

Today, our society has two underlying currents. On the one hand, attitudes of distrust and rejection towards the disabled are diminishing as our society learns to be more tolerant and open. On the other hand, we are plagued by the demons of success and power. Which parents today would welcome a disabled child, when screening is so readily available and abortion the advised option? These parents know that some people will look at them disapprovingly for bringing a child into the world that is a burden to society.

The Church must speak out and proclaim the dignity of the human person as Pope John Paul II did at every opportunity, and as Pope Benedict XVI is continuing to do. (His message to the World Day for the Sick, 2006) The Church must support all families who face daunting choices. The Church must witness that it is possible to find happiness in this life, despite trials and sufferings. Many movements, communities and associations dedicate themselves to this aim.

The "Amitié-Espérance" movement (Friendship and Hope) was founded in Lourdes in 1978, specifically to serve the needs of the mentally disabled. Its patron is the father of St Thérèse of the Child-Jesus who was himself afflicted by mental illness towards the end of his life. Friendship and prayer gatherings started in 1982, primarily for the disabled and their families, and they held their first pilgrimage in Lourdes on Ascension Day 2007. They are a living confirmation of Lourdes' mission towards people with a disability, their families and companions.

Lourdes desires to help them on their pilgrimage both here and through life. This is easier said than done: a mission is also a challenge.

PERSONAL EXPERIENCE

Valuing the difference

"I have called you by your name" (Isaiah 43, 1)

I am deeply privileged to be the Director of HCPT, the Pilgrimage Trust, at a time when pilgrimages are booming. I was a shy 13 year-old when I went on my first pilgrimage, but since then Lourdes has deeply affected my life and led me to achieve things I would never have dreamed of.

I remember the turmoil I felt inside when I went on my first HCPT trip aged 16. I was very shy, so did not believe that I could actually make friends with children who had disabilities, never mind adults. Would we be able to understand each other and if not, how would I deal with the embarrassment? Wouldn't it be easier just to leave or to cross over to the other side of the street to avoid meeting them?

At first, I hid my difficulties by trying to be entertaining and funny (usually in vain). It took me several years before I realized that it was possible to speak to a person with disabilities, whether adult or child. I managed to talk to an elderly lady who suffered from cerebral palsy and was totally unable to communicate. We did not hear the lunch bell because something far more important was taking place between us. Suddenly, I realized that, if I really tried hard, I could understand her. She told me about her life and the way in which people pretended they could understand her and how, during a pilgrimage, she had not been allowed to join in a discussion about people with disabilities because no one could understand what she was saying; people would talk around her without taking any notice of her as though she was stupid. Suddenly I thought to check whether she had eaten her packed lunch, but she hadn't because no one had thought to help her unwrap it. That moment really taught me something.

I do not have all the answers about people with disabilities, but I believe strongly that the best way in which we give value to the differences between us, (that is, accepting that we are different, but all made in the image of God), is shown by the adults and children with disabilities, together with those who look after them, spending all their time in small groups throughout their pilgrimage. This is something HCPT insists on. Each member of the group is valued as an individual, each with their own contribution to give. It is by living together and by sharing our experiences that we can really understand each other.

In the pastoral document entitled *Valuing Difference – People with Disabilities in the Life and Mission of the Church* (1998), the bishops of England and Wales "set out both a vision and a method for enabling people with disabilities to participate fully in the life and mission of the Church."

It is those who have disabilities who are best placed to challenge our ideas, because ordinary people have a surprising lack of sensitivity as the following examples will show.

Lack of sensitivity

Does he take sugar? was a BBC radio programme about the difficulties linked to being disabled. Afraid or embarrassed in case they were not understood, the person would direct their question to the carer instead of to the disabled person. This highlights clearly what so many disabled people resent: being treated like inanimate objects and not like people in their own right.

"What time did you put them to bed?" asked a colleague to a nurse who had just come back from Lourdes.

"Whenever they want!" she replied.

"She looked at me as though I was somebody"

Each one of us has been created in the image and likeness of God and is loved by him. Each one of us is a human being who has the right to be treated with dignity.

The Blessed Virgin gave us a magnificent example of the friendly way in which she spoke to Bernadette, young, weak and illiterate: "Please would you be so kind as to come here for fifteen days." There was nothing condescending in the manner in which she spoke. Her smile was pure. She spoke to Bernadette with courtesy, as though she were her equal. Bernadette was surprised at being addressed with such respect, perhaps for the first time in her life. She told the priests almost incredulously: "She looked at me as though I was somebody." Each person, with or without disabilities deserves that same respect.

A biblical inspiration

Each one of us is also unique. We have a name, which, more than anything else, says who we are. It is our identity. I always respond warmly when someone remembers my name. I feel appreciated. I remember Zaccheus's joy when Jesus called him by name. What a gift! We are called by name; called by the Blessed Virgin to join in the procession, called by God to be a person in our own right. God has chosen me, just as I am. As a name for our mission therefore I requested the biblical phrase "I have called you by your name" (Isaiah 42, 1).

Bernadette – patron saint of people with "special needs"

In the United Kingdom, we use the expression "special needs" to describe a difficulty, whether it be physical, emotional or educational, particularly with reference to children. Some would say that Bernadette was a child with "special needs", because of her very basic schooling and precarious state of health. She herself experienced living with disability and with social misfortune. Yet she was equally and truly a human being: sometimes a bit simple, but never pretentious and always with a sense of humour.

Our patron saint is therefore St Bernadette. Her humanity, her humility, her total acceptance of what God wanted for her, just like the Blessed Virgin, speaks to the very depth of our being. The badge that HCPT pilgrims wear is the image of

St Bernadette, a young girl wearing clogs and carrying a rosary. The Blessed Virgin stands behind her, reassuring her, welcoming us with open arms and leading us to her Son. The two of them together are our inspiration.

Richard King

CHAPTER EIGHT

THE MISSION OF THE CHURCH
AND THE NATIONS

The vocation of the Church is to be universal. "Go and make disciples of all the nations" (Matthew 28, 19).

In the Bible, the word "nation" does not have a political connotation. By contrast today, in France, (as well as other countries) the nation's identity has almost divine status; it is always spelt with a capital "N", and one of the biggest squares in Paris is named after it – Place de la Nation.

The meaning of "universal" in the Old Testament

In the Old Testament, the word "nations" or "gentiles" (from the Latin word *gentes*) refers to "peoples outside Israel", collectively known as pagans. Already in the Old Testament we see that God's call is not limited to Israel. Holy figures such as Abel and Noah lived before Israel even existed. There were other holy men and women too, who were in fact "pagans" because they came from outside Israel: the High Priest Melchisedech; Jethro, stepfather of Moses; Uri the Hittite, whom David killed in order to steal his wife; Naaman the Syrian, whom Elijah cured of leprosy; not to mention women like Rahab, who helped to capture Jericho; the Queen of Sheba who recognised the wisdom of Solomon; and Ruth who refused to leave her stepmother Naomi and return to her own people, " Your people will be my people and your God will be my God" (Ruth 1, 16).

The prophets, and Isaiah in particular, announce that Jerusalem shall call all pagans to itself: "Come, Let us go up to the mountain of Yahweh, to the house of the God of Jacob... for the Law will issue from Zion and the word of Yahweh from Jerusalem" (Isaiah 2, 2-3). The Lord prepares a banquet for all peoples. (Isaiah 25, 6) and says to Israel: "Widen the space of your tent" (Isaiah 54, 2). In Jesus' time, "the square of the gentiles" was still under construction at the entrance to the Temple as a clear gesture by Herod of openness to other peoples.

In the story of Babel, God creates confusion amongst different languages in preparation for a single harmony of thought. Humanity is not split into different peoples as a punishment. It is God who divides his people, "giving them their own inheritance", and fixing their boundaries. For himself, he chose Israel: "Yahweh's portion was his people" (Deuteronomy 32, 8-9). But every single person, no matter what nation he belongs to, whether Lebanese, Palestinian, or Ethiopian, can call himself a child of Jerusalem:

"Look at Tyre, Philistia, Ethiopia,
so and so was born there."

But of Zion it will be said,
"Everyone was born there."

(Psalm 87, 4-5)

Judaism was certainly not indifferent to other peoples. At the time of Jesus, the number of Jews living outside of Israel was about 5 million, as opposed to 3 million living in the Holy Land. The Bible had already been translated into Greek (the Septuagint). Up until the destruction of the Temple in the year 70 every Jew and every pagan sympathetic to Judaism, had to "Go up to Jerusalem" each year for the three great pilgrimages. Jesus did so himself. The Psalm quoted above ends with the words "All make their home in you". Everything is centred on Jerusalem. Each year, the Passover pilgrims yearn to be able "to return once again to Jerusalem next year".

Catholic means more than universal

Jesus reverses the whole process. He does not instruct his disciples to bring all pagans to Jerusalem, but instead to carry the Gospel beyond Jerusalem, to Judea, Samaria and "even to the ends of the earth" (Acts 1, 8). The Acts of the Apostles recount how the Gospel spread, particularly to Rome (as the centre of the Empire), where the two pillars of the Church, Peter and Paul, were martyred.

It is a pity that Christianity is not closer to its Jewish roots. It is also a pity that we do not know very much about how the Gospel spread to other areas beyond the Mediterranean Basin. It is enough to say that Rome has never replaced Jerusalem. The Crusades did not have a good reputation regarding the Orthodox and Muslims and are still a source of contention. One thing a Catholic can never say about Rome is: "All shall make their home in you". The most he or she will be able to say is that "All roads lead to Rome".

The Catechism of the Catholic Church, published at the request of John Paul II, specifies that "the Church is Catholic in a double sense" (830) and that both meanings imply "total". "First, the Church is Catholic because Christ is present in her... she receives from him the fullness of the means of salvation." (Sadly her members do not always use these means). "Secondly, the Church is Catholic because she has been sent out by Christ on a mission to the whole human race." Since the human race is not only numerous but infinitely varied, the Catholic Church both dwells within and grows from many smaller "Particular Churches", to use a key-phrase of Vatican II, based on Tradition (LG 23).

What is meant by "Particular Churches?" They refer to our dioceses. Each diocese is not simply a piece of the Church, like a piece of a huge jigsaw puzzle, or a small cog in a mechanism that covers the whole world. "The Particular Churches are fully Catholic through their communion with one of them, the Church of Rome, which presides in charity" (CCC 834). Then follows a quotation from Ireneus, saint and bishop of Lyons in the 2nd century: "For with this Church, by reason of its pre-eminence, the whole Church, that is the faithful everywhere, must necessarily be in accord."

Since our present Pope Benedict XVI is an accomplished musician, forgive me for comparing the Church to an orchestra: the Church of Rome, and therefore the Bishop of Rome, plays the first violin and not the conductor.

110

The international vocation of Lourdes

The international vocation of Lourdes came about early on, helped by the arrival of the railway. Unmistakably part of France but a long way from Paris, the Bigorre region enjoys all the special characteristics of being close to the border and set amidst mountains.

During the 19th century, the greatest number of pilgrims who came from outside France, were Belgian. They travelled across France by train, taking not much longer than the same journey does today. The first Belgian pilgrimage dates back to 1873. It is more difficult to travel by train from Spain, because the railway gauge is different on either side of the Pyrenees.

Different from other shrines such as Fatima, Our Lady of Pilar in Zaragoza, or Jasna Gora in Czsetochowa, it is possible to come to Lourdes without any knowledge at all of the History of France or even of Europe. Mary does not speak to Bernadette about current events, nor about the potato crop as at La Salette. Lourdes remains outside of a particular period of history.

From the outset, the international characteristic of Lourdes was highlighted by its unique link with Rome. How could Pope Pius IX and his successors not interpret the name the Lady finally revealed to Bernadette as an approbation of the Dogma of the Immaculate Conception? Through its special link with the successor of Peter, who represents the source of unity for all Particular Churches, Lourdes is also linked in a special way to the Particular Churches, and for this reason the feast of Our Lady of Lourdes appears in the liturgical calendar of the Universal Church.

It was in Lourdes that Pope John Paul II celebrated the first World Day for the Sick, announcing the next one to be held in 2004. Up until then there had been many international eucharistic and Marian congresses in Lourdes. Pope John Paul was due to preside at the congress in 1981 but the assassination attempt prevented him from going, and he was represented by Cardinal Gantin. The Centenary of Lourdes in 1958 was marked by the Marian congress, presided over by Cardinal Tisserant. It will be the same for the Jubilee in 2008.

Another example of a gathering in Lourdes on a world wide scale was in 1935 at the end of the Jubilee of the Redemption, attended by Cardinal Pacelli, (later Pope Pius XII) whilst he was still Secretary of State, closest collaborator to the Pope. On that occasion it was peace that drew many together in unity, but the international dimension of Lourdes also developed as a result of war. In 1934, 60,000 war veterans from 19 different countries gathered at Lourdes in an endeavour to avert war. Two years later they came in even greater numbers from 20 countries. These two pilgrimages became the forerunners of the International Military Pilgrimage held annually. During these pilgrimages, visitors to Lourdes not only hear different languages being spoken, but also see uniforms representing different countries, including the Swiss Guards.

Another international pilgrimage is that of the Knights of Malta. They have been coming for fifty years. Like the Vatican they are involved in diplomatic relations with a large number of countries and have representatives on a number of international bodies. Throughout its long history, the Order has been composed of seven language groups, representing seven kingdoms: Provence, Auvergne, France, Italy, Aragon, England and Germany. Today their pilgrimage is not only international but intercontinental.

Lourdes welcomes individual pilgrims and groups from Europe and all over the world. There is nothing original about this, but what is remarkable is how long this has been going on. The visible witness of gifts, banners, and *ex-votos* can be found

112

at the shrine or at the Musée-Trésor, whilst others are conserved as patrimony. In 1878 the diocese of Rio de Janeiro offered the gift of a chalice, in atonement for desecrating the image of Lourdes during a carnival in 1876, the year in which the basilica of the Immaculate Conception was consecrated: Lourdes was still young at the time but its reputation had already reached the whole world.

The international dimension of Lourdes became even more evident during the Centenary of 1958. Already familiar with air travel, Lourdes airport had been welcoming charter flights for some time. During the Centenary year, many international pilgrimages were held, including the pilgrimage for workers, and in 1960 the first world congress for young farmers.

There are also many "little Lourdes", reaching beyond Lourdes itself. In the 19th century, the spreading of the message of Lourdes was taken up by a great many men and women religious who left France to go and be missionaries. There are countless numbers of grottos outside Europe, as well as shrines, parishes and institutions that carry the name of Lourdes.

Babel and Pentecost

How does Lourdes help to make so many pilgrims from all over the world feel at home? Everything is available in 6 official languages: French, Italian, English, Spanish, German and Dutch. These languages are used throughout ceremonies and processions, in the welcome centres and in all the printed information.

There are also chaplains from the Oblates of Mary Immaculate who are native speakers in one or other of the official languages and assist as language co-ordinators.

Amongst their international community there are also many other chaplains who are not French or even European.

Lourdes is well known for its repertoire of multilingual singing and international Masses which are celebrated every Sunday and Wednesday so that every pilgrim who spends several days in Lourdes can participate. In the summer there are also international Masses for young people.

A more spiritual aspect of being Catholic can be found in the underground Basilica, where, around the walls, many saints from different nations are depicted, including Albania, Chile and Uganda. This is keeping with the work of Pope John Paul II. In order to feel truly "Church", every nation needs to "generate" bishops, and find identity with the saints, particularly with saints from their own land. In every country he visited, John Paul II beatified and canonised local saints. It was his way of practising "inculturation". Benedict XVI followed his example, when on his visit to Brazil in 2007, he beatified a Brazilian Fransciscan.

It is our duty to respect the culture of each and every person, of which language plays such a big part, so that everyone may grow in unity. At Pentecost the great sign witnessed by the crowd was that everyone could hear the wonders of God proclaimed in their own language. Lourdes can witness to the Church how to welcome visitors from all over the world in a language they can understand, making it possible for them to participate together in the same celebrations, particularly the Mass and daily processions.

However, the actual number of pilgrims from different countries who manage to dialogue in any depth with one another is still relatively few. The helpers are more likely to do so. The international service we give is still modest. This proves all the more that the attraction of Lourdes goes beyond the language barrier, especially where young people are concerned.

In order to be truly Catholic, Lourdes must be well integrated within its own diocese, the diocese of Tarbes, and within its own country, France. To be Catholic also means to put down roots. Lourdes is not a wandering planet lost in space where life has nothing to do with everything else going on around it.

It is important to make an international link between Lourdes and other great Marian shrines. With this aim in mind, we have composed a rosary, not of 20 mysteries, but of 20 Marian shrines: Altötting (Germany), Banneux (Belgium), Brezje (Slovenia), Csiksomlyo (Romania), Czestochowa (Poland), Einsiedeln (Switzerland), Fatima (Portugal), Gibraltar (the shrine of Our Lady of Europe), Knock (Ireland), Levoca (Slovakia), Loreto (Italy), Lourdes (France), Mariapoch (Hungary), Mariazell (Austria), Marija Bistrica (Croatia), Malta, Vilnius (Lithuania), Walsingham (England), Zaragoza (Spain).

This forms the European Marian Network. Each shrine is original and we have so much to learn. This too is what "Catholic" means. There are more great shrines to Mary in other continents. When will we form the Universal Network of Mary?

The Church's mission among nations

I have lived most of my life in Argentina in a town at the foot of the Andes. It was there that I heard the message of Lourdes for the first time when I was five years old. My parents had sent me to a school run by the French Missionaries of the Immaculate Conception of Lourdes. The priests introduced me to the story of the Apparitions of the Blessed Virgin and to the story of Bernadette. They helped me and many other young people discover that trying to live Mary's words ourselves was the same as being there in Lourdes with her. With their wisdom and simplicity they revealed to us the treasures of the Gospel. Their teaching through my childhood and adolescence has remained imprinted on my heart forever.

These French religious, like many others, in faithfulness to the Church of their times and the Missionary outreach of the

19th century, preached the Gospel by means of three main devotions which are known the world over: the Sacred Heart, Thérèse of the Child Jesus and Our Lady of Lourdes. If you add to that the great devotion that the people of South America already had towards Our Lady, inherited from the Spanish missionaries, then you understand just how important a place Our Lady of Lourdes holds in the hearts of the peoples of the South American continent.

A few years later, as an ordained priest and religious of the Order of the Immaculate Conception, I myself had the grace of being sent to France as a chaplain to the shrine. There I was able to discover and live my priestly ministry and through my duties and responsibilities, to discover many new aspects of Lourdes such as the international dimension of its message.

Living alongside pilgrims from all over the world, hearing the different languages and seeing the variety of races and cultures certainly gives Lourdes its international, universal dimension. And yet I am certain that this is only the exterior face of something much deeper that lives within the heart of every pilgrim.

At Lourdes, Mary offers Bernadette the experience of following Christ, of making her own experience as a believer. Mary sets before us a model of evangelisation that opens itself to the sacraments. Before Bernadette could make the experience her own, the message had to be sown and take root within a culture. Mary respects and takes into account Bernadette's own language, her local dialect, her family situation, her personal social and ecclesial background. Mary "incarnates" herself so to speak in the reality of this young girl, drawing close to her and welcoming her as she is. Like an echo of the Gospel, which has taken root in a particular culture, her message is, by its very nature, universal. The message of Lourdes begins with the reality of Bernadette's life and it is the same for every pilgrim. There is no need to prepare oneself to go to Lourdes, it is enough just to go there: "Come here for 15 days." What takes place at Lourdes can also happen outside Lourdes itself. As a Latin American I know thousands of people who for various reasons would never be able to go to the shrine of Lourdes, but they live "the grace" of Lourdes with great fruitfulness. When someone is speaking about Lourdes, no matter where they may be in the world, they are "in Lourdes".

Everything that surrounds the message of Lourdes is universal: the grotto, the water, the light, the crowd, the sick and those who look after them. The prayers and gestures of a pilgrimage are all easily accessible and understood. But perhaps it is Bernadette herself who speaks to us of universality; her personal situation is directly in touch with all the cultures and situations of modern man. At the heart of the frustration of her own humanity, Mary invites her to discover "another world". As a priest many people have shared with me the personal graces they have received at Lourdes: "It is different"; "Where there was darkness in my life, now there is light"; "My life has meaning"; "Jesus is the defender of my lost cause". These witnesses illustrate the words of St Paul which sum up the message of Lourdes so well: "However much sin increased, grace was always greater" (Romans 5: 20).

Over the years in which I have been a chaplain at the Shrine I have discovered another aspect of Lourdes' international dimension. All of us who work at the service of the shrine, priests, religious, lay people, and I am thinking particularly of the volunteers and those responsible for so many different tasks, first and foremost we are responsible for passing on a grace that has been given to us by the Church, and only in second place are we organisers of a shrine. Just as with the Gospel, the message of Lourdes must continually be announced and put into practice because it is a living matter, a living word, which generates life. The message of Lourdes is not simply "Come" but also "Go and tell", and grace has no boundaries.

Fr Duboé, Missionary of the Immaculate Conception of Lourdes, and one of the first chaplains of Lourdes, made a prophetic statement in 1866: "The future of Lourdes is the Immaculate Conception." I think that 150 years later we can say the same. Humanity that has been enlightened by the Gospel is not called to dry up, but to be fruitful like Mary, like Bernadette and so many other pilgrims, missionaries, and witnesses of the message of Lourdes scattered throughout the world.

Fr Horacio Brito
Missionary of the Immaculate Conception of Lourdes,
Former Assistant Rector and General Secretary
of the Shrine.

CHAPTER NINE

THE MISSION OF THE CHURCH
AND PEACE

Too often people associate religion with war. Current events
and history have done little to help change this opinion.
Religion is vulnerable to criticism. For believers, religion represents
what is most sacred. One of the best methods for warmongering
is to convince the troops that they are acting in the name of
God or that their religion is under threat.

To take a recent example, Islamic extremists blow themselves
up along with their victims, invoking the name of God, in
order to prevent the "unholy West" from imposing their
way of life which they maintain is so contrary to Islam.
What we associate with Islamic terrorists, we unfortunately
then associate with Islam and with religion in general.
Monotheistic religions which are founded upon a particular
revelation are the most suspect: their origins and beliefs can
foster intolerance.

Pope John Paul II was conscious of this global criticism of religion, which is difficult to deny. When war is waged in the name of religion it is a perversion of the Gospel. He was aware of the way in which religion can be instrumentalised and used as leaven to stir up mass hatred. Religious leaders should never get involved in the propaganda of war.

Can any religious group seriously say they have never succumbed to the temptation to take sides? The Catholic Church is conscious that it has not always been impartial in these matters. On the occasion of the jubilee year 2000, Pope John Paul II apologised on behalf of the Church, for the times when force was used to spread the faith.

A few years earlier he had taken the unprecedented initiative of inviting the leaders of all religions to Assisi to pray for peace. What is more, this same Pope broke his normal friendly reserve to speak out against the war in Iraq. From his Vatican window, he condemned it and, right up to the last possible minute, sought every avenue possible to avert war, including sending envoys to George W Bush and Saddam Hussein.

The Church knows that war rarely solves conflict. Instead it builds up resentment, leaving behind as much material and moral devastation for the victors as it does for the defeated. It fills up the graveyards and hospitals.

In choosing the name Benedict, our present Pope indicated that he wished to recall the actions of his predecessor Benedict XV, who endeavoured to get both sides in the First World War to reach a compromise, yet he was considered a traitor by both.

Between the two Benedicts we must not forget Pope Pius XII. It is not so well known that he permitted the Vatican to be an intermediary in the plans to eliminate Hitler. Let us not forget John XXIII's Encyclical *Pacem in terris* and Pope Paul VI's exclamation at the United Nations Assembly "No more war!"

But the Church is not pacifist without exception. It would have been immoral to let Hitler, Stalin and Mao seize world power. However, the most effective form of defence is moral force. The Berlin Wall eventually fell because lies and brainwashing could no longer withstand the truth and the courage to speak out that truth.

A long tradition of moral theology has attempted to define a just war. It is an act of self-defence, declared by a legitimate source of power, once all other options have been exhausted, and where there are good prospects of success, and in so far as is possible, without incurring human and material damage disproportionate to the original offence (to the evil to be eliminated). It is doubtful that any aggressor has ever considered the principles of the just war! We must always strive to enlighten people's consciences, even if passion blinds reason.

Limiting or preventing evil

Apart from making declarations, the Church must also engage in concrete actions. During the Middles Ages, the Church sought to establish the "Peace of God" and the "Truce of God". These restrictions were often breached, but they demonstrated the underlying conviction that war is wrong and must be kept to an absolute minimum.

Europe has been through many wars, all of them horrific. However, there are varying degrees of horror. The doctrine of the Catholic Church particularly opposes "total war", which permits the bombing of towns such as Reims in the First World War or Dresden or Hiroshima in the Second World War.

The Geneva Convention and the ban on atomic, chemical and biological weapons echoes the logic that the Church has always tried to follow: that of imposing restrictions upon war. However, as the means of destruction have increased, the teaching of the Popes and the condemnation of war have had to become stronger and clearer. War is the "ultimate failure of authentic humanism" (1st January 1999). War is a "defect of humanity" (13 January 2003).

The Church has always favoured negotiation. She upholds diplomacy, and has her own network of diplomats, the papal nuncios. In recent history she has taken part in missions of mediation.

Alas, diplomacy is often swept aside by the appetite for victory and bloodshed. That is why it is necessary to offer the opposing parties a wider framework in which to lay out their claims and grievances, using international opinion as a witness.

After the Second World War, the Catholic Church approved the foundation of The United Nations and on the occasion of its 20th anniversary, the Pope decided to visit the UN Headquarters in New York, only the second time that a Pope had travelled outside Italy in modern times. The UN has often been criticised for its inefficiency but, according to experts, the situation in the world would be much worse without it.

In an endeavour to disarm aggressors, the Catholic Church has always upheld the right to intervene, even in very delicate situations. She approves of international tribunals for war criminals, so that those guilty of atrocious war crimes cannot cling to their immunity from the State.

Lourdes throughout the turbulence of history

Beneath that shadow of her former fortress, Lourdes was living in peaceful times when the Blessed Virgin appeared to Bernadette. But history does not take long to catch up with Lourdes. In 1872, Alsace and Lorraine, recently lost by France, led a procession of 250 banners to the Basilica of the Immaculate Conception. History entered Lourdes with mourning and sorrow.

In the decades that followed, French pilgrims prayed long and hard before their territory was finally restored. Germany was not completely absent from Lourdes during that time. Groups of German pilgrims came in 1875, 1888, 1908, 1912 and 1914. In 1906, Germany presented the gift of a statue for the Way for the Cross and two German bishops attended the Eucharistic Congress in 1904.

During the 1914-18 War, Lourdes opened its hospitals to take in injured and convalescing soldiers. Once again, suffering entered Lourdes. On the first anniversary of Armistice Day, land and sea forces united in a pilgrimage to give thanks for victory and peace. They laid the first memorial stone. Each year a French pilgrimage returns to celebrate Mass and offer prayers for those killed in battle.

During the 1939-45 War, Lourdes was once again turned into a hospital. The town was spared any bloodshed by the German military commander, a Catholic, who did not wish a Marian city and place of healing to be turned into a battlefield.

Monsigneur Théas, Pax Christi and the International Military Pilgrimage

Lourdes has long been associated with peace, not only because of the memories and sufferings of war, but because of Mgr Théas, Bishop of Montauban at the time of the Second World War. In the same vein as Mgr Saliège, Archbishop of Toulouse, on Sunday 30th August 1942, he read out in person a message condemning the deportation of the Jews: "the Christian conscience" cannot approve these "anti-Semitic" measures. A few months later, in 1943, he made a public stance against Nazi death camps. Finally he complained to the Chief Commandant when his priests were badly treated by Nazi soldiers.

Within a few days, on 9 June 1944, he was arrested and transferred to the labour camp at Compiègne from where he would have been deported if he had not been freed on 24 August 1944.

Whilst being held at Compiègne, Bishop Théas led his fellow prisoners to meditate on Jesus' words "Love you enemies", encouraging them to pray for their guards. He himself offered Masses for Germany.

At the same time, in the winter of 1944, a teacher from Agen, Mme Dortel-Claudot, felt called to pray for Germany, destroyed by Nazism and bombing. She formed a small prayer group together with a war widow, the daughter of a deported Jew and some Carmelite sisters.

In 1945 she made contact with Bishop Théas and they began the "Crusade of Prayer" for Germany, under the name Pax Christi. Bishop Théas became the first national and then international leader.

In the meantime, on 16 July 1946, Bishop Théas became first administrator of Lourdes, and the following year Bishop of Tarbes and Lourdes. So it was only natural that in 1947 the first gathering for the 50 delegates of Pax Christi from six different countries, should meet in Lourdes. In 1948 they met at Kevelaer, Germany, a Marian shrine near the

Netherlands. Bishop Théas celebrated the sacrament of First Holy Communion. Fifty years later, in 1998, I was invited to Kevelaer to celebrate the jubilee of this memorable date. A large number of these children, now in their sixties, were present, which shows how much they had been marked by that occasion.

In 1948, 10,000 pilgrims from 26 nations replied to the invitation of Pax Christi and gathered in Lourdes for their first truly international pilgrimage. A permanent Pax Christi presence was opened in 1953 and an international meeting Centre was run from 1963 – 1988.

In 1958, German soldiers in uniform returned to France for the first time since the war. They came for the first international military pilgrimage which gathered together 40,000 soldiers from 14 different nations. Since then, the International Military Pilgrimage has been the most visible outward sign of the Church's mission for peace.

"My peace I give you, a peace the world cannot give"

Despite living today with the victory of the Resurrection, evil continues to be active and we have to work to achieve peace. That is why Christ said "My peace I leave you, my own peace I give you. A peace the world cannot give." The world can only give a limited kind of peace. This phrase in St John's Gospel reminds us of another phrase of Jesus: "If you who are wicked know how to give what is good to your children, how much more so does your heavenly Father…"

Because we have been given the gifts of love and reason, we have the capacity to understand that imperfect peace is worth more than a beautiful victory which leaves behind only material, demographic and spiritual ruin. France and Germany realized this in the end. On the eve of the third millennium, and World Day of Prayer, (1st January) I had the joy of concelebrating Mass at the Grotto with my fellow German priests. Yes, peace is possible. The International Military Pilgrimage, which brings together the armies of countries who have often fought each other, even recently, is a strong and visible witness.

Peace

Allowing a former soldier to speak about peace to mark the Jubilee anniversary of Lourdes, is evidence to me of how much more today soldiers are associated with peace keeping. The collapse of the Soviet Empire 15 years ago marked the end of a polarised world. In its wake it left our planet in a state of armed peace, or as Raymond Aron called it, "the era of aggressive peace", in which war has many new and different guises.

The situation became characterised by the permanent management of multiple and complex crises in which the armed forces worked closely with those on the political, economic and humanitarian front to put an end to conflicts generated by the resurgence of "nationalist extremism" exacerbated by ethnic and religious differences.

Receiving their mandate from the international community, the army became peace keepers. Naturally, in the use of force, they still played the principle role in bringing about a ceasefire or bringing perpetrators to order. However, they also participated in the stabilisation and reconstruction phase, not only maintaining peace by their very presence, but also working in partnership along the long and difficult road back to normality. This period is decisive in the battle to consolidate peace.

This fight is all the more difficult because it demands from those involved a thorough understanding and knowledge of the current situation for even the most basic level of action; for example the perfect mastering of the use of force delegated to them by governments. Acting more and more on the side of those who have become hostages or victims of crises, they find themselves living alongside them, sharing their distress and their misery in which more often than not they are the only ones who can bring some relief. Confronted with the possibility of violent death, like their predecessors, they appreciate the true value of civil peace and the need to safeguard it.

Committed to fighting for peace with the use of arms, risking their own lives, they are asked to intervene in conflicts and promote reconciliation and peace between local fighting factions. They prove their own capacity to overcome past antagonisms by uniting their efforts to the very centre of multi-national coalitions; the enemies of yesterday, the enemies in the cold war, seek mutual understanding in order to give back the priceless gift of peace to the people who have had it taken away from them or never known it.

It is in Lourdes, during the International Military Pilgrimage that this faith of soldiers from all the countries of the world in this mission as peacemakers is expressed in a very special way. Alongside the French soldiers and their traditional allies, there is always a great number of Germans. And for 15 years now, representatives of the Eastern Bloc armies, who for 45 years opposed them on the other side of the Iron Curtain, march together in close ranks during the pilgrimage.

The need to come before Our Lady of Lourdes to pray together is all the more apparent with the presence, over the last 5 years, of a delegation of the international security forces deployed in Kosovo; these men and women who fight for peace in the Balkans, also take part each year in a Marian pilgrimage, like that of Lourdes, in Kosovo; at Lesnica they join with Kosovan Catholics to pray for peace at the shrine of the Blessed Virgin that Mother Teresa often used to visit when she was young.

Whether in Lourdes or in Lesnica, the soldiers of the 21st century seek Mary's intercession to help them win the battles for peace which they are fighting in increasingly difficult conditions; they certainly deserve to be called peace keeping soldiers.

General Marcel Valentin

131

CHAPTER TEN

THE MISSION OF THE CHURCH NOURISHED BY THE EUCHARIST

This chapter could be considered the most important of all, because the Eucharist is so essential to our faith, and because Bernadette longed to make her First Communion just prior to the apparitions. It had only been two weeks since she had left Bartrès and returned to Lourdes when the apparitions began. Why had she been so determined to return to the cachot, to the hovel that was her home? She missed her family, certainly, but above all she was determined not to miss the start of her First Communion classes.

Bernadette finally made her First Holy Communion on 3 June 1858 at the chapel of the Sisters of Nevers who ran the school as well as the hospice at Lourdes. Her parish priest, who had been convinced since 25 March that Bernadette was telling the truth, allowed her to make it despite her very poor knowledge of the catechism. He has left a beautiful testimony of Bernadette's behaviour on the days leading up to her First Holy Communion and on the day itself.

As for Bernadette, she avoided the trap of trying to make comparisons between First Communion and the apparitions: "They go together, but they cannot be compared. They have both made me very happy," she said.

"You cannot compare them"

The apparitions at Lourdes are unique, whereas Holy Communion is meant for everyone. Bernadette was the only one to see and hear Our Lady, but there was nothing out of the ordinary about her taking Communion along with everyone else, apart from her exceptional devotion.

At the grotto Bernadette had a vision. At Mass she only saw the same host that we all see briefly at the moment of elevation by the priest. St Thomas Aquinas said that not only Christ's divinity but also his humanity is hidden within the host.

The Eucharist is celebrated by the ministry of the priesthood but the apparitions go beyond the Magisterium of the Church, which can only make its pronouncement after the event.

The apparitions are temporary. There was only one more after Bernadette had made her First Communion. It was a pure gift from God that the Lady asked Bernadette to come and see her everyday for two weeks, out of which there were two days when she did not appear. By contrast, Bernadette had special permission to receive Communion as often as she wanted, either at Nevers or at Lourdes

"They are two things which go together"

Bernadette did not say any more than this. It is a pity because for our brothers and sisters from other Christian traditions, this is such an important part of their understanding Lourdes. Both Holy Communion and the apparitions are a hymn of praise to the Most Holy Trinity. Every time Bernadette returned to the grotto, she recited the Rosary, beginning every decade with the Our Father and ending with the Glory Be, spoken in her own dialect. Bernadette recounts that Our Lady moved only her fingers during the Hail Mary, but moved her lips when it came to the Glory Be. In the same way, the eucharistic prayer is addressed to the Father but ends in praise of the Trinity: "Through him (Christ), with him, in him, to you almighty Father, in unity with the Holy Spirit all glory and honour are yours..."

In each case, Bernadette is in communion with the passion of Christ, obviously in the Eucharist, which celebrates the death and resurrection of the Lord, but also during the apparitions. Four times, on and after 24 February, Bernadette performs humiliating and disfiguring gestures in imitation of the Suffering Servant (Isaiah 53) of whom Christ is the perfect fulfilment.

Bernadette performed these gestures "for sinners", just as Christ poured out his blood for the forgiveness of sins.

At the Grotto and during Communion, Bernadette experienced such an intimacy that she was able to confide in Our Lady things that we shall never know, things which she kept secret between her and the Lady, such as the thoughts in her mind and heart on the day of her First Communion.

The Mass is communitarian. At the Grotto, only Bernadette was able to see and hear Our Lady, although from the second apparition onwards she was always accompanied by others praying with her.

And finally, was not the Eucharist the foretaste of that other world in which the Lady had promised she would be happy?

Someone who perhaps knew Bernadette best, Father Ravier, wrote a little book on the place that the Eucharist held in Bernadette's life, how she compares herself to a grain of wheat ground by the millstone. It is not the purpose here to study this little book, but it serves to remind us of the link that has always existed between Lourdes and the Eucharist.

The churches at Lourdes

From the first moment after the apparitions had been recognised, Mass was celebrated in the grotto at a makeshift altar. Since then there have been many altars and it is interesting to compare them to see in what ways our devotion to the Eucharist and our taste in design have evolved over 150 years.

The chapels and the churches also followed. On 2 March, Bernadette carried the message to the parish priest that the Lady wanted a chapel to be built, "even if it's just a small one," Bernadette added, to try and encourage them. The next day the priest replied that if the Lady would kindly let them know her name and make the rosebush flower then "yes, he would build her chapel and it wouldn't be small!" He kept his word, even though it was not he who took charge of the building work.

The design of all the churches, the crypt, the upper and lower basilicas, the church of St Bernadette and St Joseph, reflect the different perceptions of the Eucharist. In the 19th century buildings the altar is at the front, preceded by choir stalls occupied by the clergy: today the layout is no longer the same but it is easy to imagine it. The St Pius X Basilica (lower basilica) was a real revolution at the time, not only because it was underground and had a capacity of 25,000, but above all because of the position of its altar, in the centre very simply surrounded by steps. As for the more recent constructions they form a semi-circle with the altar in the centre. Everything is curved.

We can find theological meaning in each of the different designs. The 19th century design, one that had been traditional in the West for centuries, symbolises Christ at the head of his Church. In the Pius X Basilica, Christ is at the heart of the community. More recently, situated in the centre of a semi-circle, the altar, and therefore Christ, unites his body.

The Eucharistic celebration, the Blessed Sacrament procession and adoration

When very large gatherings take place, which exceed the capacity of the basilicas, then it is necessary to celebrate outdoors. The archives hold photographs of these momentous occasions on the Esplanade, where the central altar was constructed on a podium, surrounded by many smaller altars where priests quietly celebrated Mass simultaneously with the principal celebrant. It is perhaps not surprising that the then Bishop of Tarbes and Lourdes, Bishop Théas, intervened at the Second Vatican Council in 1962 in favour of concelebration. After trying it first in the monasteries, it seems that the first publicly concelebrated Mass in France, took place in Lourdes on 26 July 1964. It was such an important moment that Lourdes requested the support of Rome.

The daily blessing of the sick began in the 1880s and from it grew the need for a procession of the Blessed Sacrament. A number of healings are attributed to this moment of the Blessed Sacrament procession. Just as many cried out to Jesus as he made his way through the Holy Land, "Master, let me see again. Lord have pity on me," so too many lift up their cries to Christ in the Eucharist.

The procession descends from the upper basilica using the ramps outside the Rosary Basilica continuing as far as the Esplanade. This image of the Church as the travelling People of God, the Pilgrim Church, became popular after Vatican II and so the procession took on a new significance of which the sick are very much a part. They are part of the Body of Christ, and he makes them one with his Church. He walks with his Church along the path of history. At key points along this journey many practical questions and questions of principle have been raised: can the sick participate with the other ordinary pilgrims? Should the priests process together near the Eucharist, or should they remain in the midst of their diocese?

At certain moments the very principle of having a procession was in abeyance. But Lourdes stood its ground and today devotion to the Eucharist has taken on new momentum, particularly adoration of the Blessed Sacrament. A special dialogue took place on the Eucharist to mark the Jubilee 2000. Continuous adoration of the Eucharist throughout the day was first introduced by the religious congregation Daughters of the Church, who came to Lourdes at the time of the centenary.

Adoration originally took place in the Rosary Chapel, then in the Pax Christi Chapel of the Pius X Basilica. In 1995 a special chapel dedicated to adoration of the Blessed Sacrament was added to the church of St Bernadette. It has no altar, so that it may be reserved totally for silence and private prayer. The Eucharist is placed in a column, resembling the column of fire which accompanied the people of Israel when they crossed the desert.

Since the year 2000, a large marquee has made it possible to accommodate a greater number of pilgrims and groups who wish to spend adoration time together. What attracts them, and in particular the young people? It is not a "restoration" of exposition, since many are discovering it for the first time. Perhaps it is due to the fact that the age in which we live needs images and a living presence and the Blessed Sacrament is both the image and presence of the Risen One.

The eucharistic processions are harder to comprehend. Many who join in because they are there at the time it starts, have little appreciation of the real presence.

Lourdes has named its biggest basilica after St Pope Pius X, who remains in history as the pope who made it possible to receive Communion often and for children to receive Communion.

He described Lourdes as "the most glorious of eucharistic thrones in the Catholic universe". Love for the Eucharist has always been evident at Lourdes, in many different ways: in its history, in its buildings, in its celebrations.

It would take too long to list all the great moments in the history of the Eucharist at Lourdes. I have indicated the main ones in the chapter "The mission of the Church and the nations".

Can Lourdes help pilgrims nourish themselves with the Eucharist?

There are many ways to express liturgy, which sometimes creates tensions. Lourdes enjoys an enviable peace in this regard. The Catholic Church lives out its universal dimension through the celebration of international Masses. It is one thing to know that the Church is spread all over the world, but another thing to experience it in reality. Those who have attended large gatherings in St Peter's Square will feel at home. It is a valuable experience to have in the age of globalisation. At Lourdes there are also some very simple celebrations of the Eucharist, held in the Grotto in the early hours of the morning or every evening at 11 pm. This diversity is very helpful in that it prevents the mystery of the Eucharist from being associated with a particular style of liturgy, be it grandiose or intimate.

On the eve of his passion, Christ instituted the Eucharist but he also washed his apostles' feet. The meaning is the same: Christ the servant of God is the servant of all, offering his life. So too at Lourdes the Eucharist is celebrated in the midst of those who are sick and those who serve them: the two dimensions are united. Young people love to serve: Lourdes is a way of helping them discover Christ who, through the Eucharist, unites us to his sacrifice.

Lourdes has never diminished its eucharistic devotion. Pope John Paul II and Pope Benedict XVI both reminded us of its value. Lourdes has the special task of making sure that there is always a strong link between eucharistic devotion and the celebration of the Eucharist. Amongst the different forms that eucharistic devotion can take, adoration is particularly appreciated. It is not something to be suspicious of, nor be too rigorous about, for many it leads to the discovery of silent prayer. The directors of the shrine and of the pilgrimages are there to assist and nourish all those who come to do adoration and to safeguard against any malpractices. Even though it is a form of personal prayer, it is still necessary to educate people in its practice. It is also important that adoration does not take the place of the eucharistic procession which is rich in biblical, ecclesial and spiritual meaning.

Lourdes also affirms the link that exists between the Eucharist and reconciliation, offering many possibilities for penance and reconciliation. The sacrament of reconciliation is widely available. More can be done to help those whose visit is brief, but who are no less pilgrims entitled to the rewards of the sacrament which they have neglected for a long time. At Lourdes reconciliation does not only happen within. The relationships between pilgrims are much more fraternal than in everyday life, despite obstacles.

Lourdes is the privileged place to attend the school of Mary, "woman of the Eucharist", just as the life of Bernadette, Mary's confidante, was completely absorbed by the Eucharist. Mary, Mother of God, was Bernadette's catechist, preparing her for her First Communion. In Western Catholicism there are two contradictory attitudes towards the Eucharist. On the one hand there are those who value it so strongly that it overshadows all other practices of Christian piety; on the other hand the huge majority of Catholics have lapsed or, in the case of young people, have never known the experience of gathering round the Eucharistic table. What if Mary, mother of Jesus could grant them a longing for the Eucharist! And what if Lourdes where she dwells, could help her in this task!

Lourdes and the Eucharist

About 40 years ago I went to Mass on the feast of Our Lady's birthday in the underground basilica. I was sitting behind the podium where the bishops were celebrating Mass and as I contemplated the long entrance procession which seemed never-ending and heard the singing of the choir and congregation, it was so moving that I felt caught up in the procession entering the heavenly Jerusalem: a moment of eternity. I have never forgotten that experience; it is similar to the union with God that I felt when I bathed in the pool, or encountered a sick person, or even a volunteer or simple pilgrim. Lourdes is a church gathered around its mother, just as it must have been for the apostles when, on returning from their mission, they gathered round to witness Mary's assumption into heaven. The joy of the Resurrection is already ours to live.

In the Eucharist we share in the sacrifice of the cross, and the presence of the sick in the front rows, reminds us that suffering is a reality, but also that it is an offering that bears fruit in the friendship and joy being shared. Suffering is overcome, the cross flows into the Resurrection. Mary's invisible presence sustains our act of faith as she unites her children so often separated.

Several years later, I found myself responsible for the Welcome Centre for Young People at the shrine and took part in the first international Mass which was celebrated in the meadow. On a smaller scale, I experienced the same reality: young people, sick and well, different languages, horizons, ages, backgrounds, cultures, and levels of faith, all invited by the same God to share in his gift of Communion. Yes, he gave his life so that we could live in him. He transforms life and many young people accept his invitation to follow him.

The body of Christ, and the body of the sick

If your heart is open, you can see many visions at Lourdes: the little man in his motorised buggy which he activates with the help of an artificial device attached to the stump where his arm should have been. He has no arms or legs, only his head and his body, but his smile radiates joy like a living host, a Eucharistic vision! In the bodies of the sick, transfigured by the grace of love shared among us, we recognise in a special way the body of Christ.

Ever since pilgrimages began it has always been possible to remain close to the presence of Jesus in the host even after Mass has ended by carrying the Blessed Sacrament in processions along the paths we tread as men and women.

Pilgrims too numerous to count have gathered outside the basilica in order to receive the blessing of the Lord, their cries bursting from their hearts as they did once in the Holy Land: "Lord, let me see; let me walk." And the miracles are repeated! The eucharistic procession has gradually become a daily event surviving even the concerns of those who viewed it as a superstitious practice linked to a sacred object used for more than it was designed for.

Those responsible for the eucharistic Congress in Lourdes in 1981 decided to suspend the procession and place the Blessed Sacrament in the more remote Chapel of Carmel, only accessible by steps. By contrast today, the Chapel of Adoration is right in the middle of the meadow surrounding the shrine. A true source of peace, healing and hearts gathered together.

Sacrament of charity

One more vision I wish to evoke is the celebration of Mass on Maundy Thursday night during the international pilgrimage of Faith & Light. A pitcher and ewer was placed at the end of each pew in the Pope Pius X Basilica, to wash the feet of the congregation. No sooner had their feet been washed than the sick rose from their seats, gathering around the podium where the altar stood, expressing their joy and recognition at this act of fraternity. From this simple ritual, life gushed forth. The sacrament of the host is at one and the same time the sacrament of our neighbour.

It is not confined to a separate place. The gift of God, the fruit of the Earth, and the work of humankind come together in the Eucharist. In the Eucharist, the material universe welcomes the power of God himself. Young people today are amongst those who recognise, or at least intuit, a host which radiates outwards. When I was responsible for the School of the Gospel, in my sabbatical year, I gathered together a group of 20 young people between the ages of 18-30. They asked me to make it possible for them to have exposition and adoration of the Blessed Sacrament; they wanted to draw from the source of Life.

Without this loving contemplation, the welcoming of our neighbour quickly gives way to measuring and calculating and fatigue. Without God's love, people have only enough energy that comes from their own human efforts. Bernadettte knew how to let herself be guided by Mary to her First Communion. Then Mary sent her back to serving the daily needs of others. Our meeting with our neighbour and our meeting with God sustain each other mutually. The patients cared for at the hospice receive and radiate light from above.

Fr André Cabes

CHAPTER ELEVEN

THE MISSION OF THE CHURCH
AND INTER-FAITH DIALOGUE

It is only comparatively recently that Christians have become aware of inter-religious dialogue as part of the Church's mission. The Fathers of the Church preferred to dialogue with philosophers rather than with other religions, following the example of St Paul.

When Saint Paul addressed the church of Athens at the Aeropagus, he observed how "extremely scrupulous they were in religious matters" (Acts 17, 22). Yet he spoke to them in philosophical terms rather than religious language: it is wrong to worship idols because God is not a material reality. Wise men listened to everything Paul had to say, except when it came to the Resurrection. At Lystra, where Paul and Barnabas had cured a cripple, they risked being taken for gods. Sacrifices had already been prepared by the time Paul intervened to prevent this unenlightened religious practice (Acts 14). In

Ephesus, the sale of small statues of Artemis provided a source of income for the town. A riot broke out with cries of "Artemis is the greatest". Fortunately, the civil authorities restored calm to the situation (Acts, 19). Religious practices do not necessarily lead to faith.

Too early for dialogue

For the first few centuries Christianity did not come into contact with other major religions. As the Roman Empire expanded, it became the official religion within and beyond the Mediterranean Basin, but it was still only in its infancy, and Christian writers at the time did not see this as very significant. Religion was a means to enshrine political power – after all, it was the emperors who had decided to persecute Christians.

Compared to the state religion, the philosophy of Plato and others seemed very attractive. Some of Plato was so wonderful that the Fathers considered him to have been inspired by Moses.

We must treat relations with Judaism separately. These relations are polemical because they exist within the same family of faith. Jews and Christians believe in the same promises (The Old Testament). Are these beliefs fulfilled in Jesus and who is Jesus? That is the question.

When Islam appeared, it replaced Christianity in the territories it conquered. The circumstances were hardly appropriate for dialogue, and when Christians found some of their own patrimony contained in the Qu'ran, it felt like a misappropriation of their property. There have been memorable moments of dialogue, such as St Francis of Assisi with the Sultan, in 1219; that of the Emperor Manuel II with the wise

Persian at the end of the 14th century, a conversation made infamous by Pope Benedict XVI.

At the time of the conquest of the Americas, the Church was criticised for not having respected the indigenous cultures, though to be fair these cultures were often bloody. As for African customs, many of them were strongly characterised by fear and dependency.

In more recent times, in Asia, Christianity came into contact with other major religions. This was unfamiliar territory. These Far East religions were impressive on account of their age, the quality of their writings, the spirituality of their "saints" and their wise men and their extensive outreach. Religious men and women from the West entered into a deep dialogue with them, especially in India.

The second half of this century completely changed the nature of the problem. Muslims settled in ever greater numbers in western countries and Islam expanded in various forms, a subject that we cannot enter into in this book. The religions of the Far East no longer reached us only through books but also through the movement of populations. Mosques were built in our towns and in the countryside Tibetan monasteries were opened. Conversions took place between one religion and another.

Vatican II, John Paul II and Benedict XVI

The Second Vatican Council marked a turning point in the way other religions were viewed. Instead of being viewed from a negative perspective, the Council recognised their dignity and called for respect towards them. The Council re-emphasized an old tradition according to which the frontiers of salvation did not coincide with belonging to the Church. Before that, salvation, it was thought, was only obtained in spite of belonging to a non-Christian religion, rather than through belonging to it.

Pope John-Paul II went a step further by announcing that religious institutions themselves should guide their faithful in the right direction, through the written word, prayer, devotions, or moral principles.

Besides the mix of races and peoples which naturally leads to dialogue about statutes, customs and traditions, sometimes tragic events also force us to engage in dialogue. Many conflicts use religion to justify situations which can end up irreconcilable. This is one of the main reasons why people are against religion.

The prophetic figure of John-Paul II, through the Assisi Peace initiative, wished to reverse this regrettable reasoning. Here religious leaders could come together, not to fight, but to pray, in a way that would not deny their true identity. You cannot ask a Muslim to recite the "Our Father" nor a Christian to venerate Vishnu. Prayers suitable for everyone to recite would have had to be vague and abstract, instead of prayer being what it truly is, the deepest expression of our religious beliefs. Instead by coming together to share our different prayers, we learn to respect each others' way of praying.

Pope Benedict XVI followed in the footsteps of his predecessor when he visited the Blue Mosque in Istanbul and spent time in silent recollection. He did not recite a Christian prayer in a Muslim edifice, nor did he publicly join in any Muslim prayers. He prayed openly, but in silence. His minute of prayer was comparable to that of John Paul II in front of the Wailing Wall in Jerusalem.

Inter-religious encounter is an essential element in today's world. The plurality of religions is here to stay. Even those who are not religious feel the effect of this reality. Without question religion has an impact upon the future of our societies and world peace. French secularism has dismissed religion as a private matter and still lives in this blindness.

On this wide open pathway between religions, Lourdes has its own part to play, for two reasons.

How Mary is perceived by others

Firstly, the faithful of other religions who come to Lourdes do so out of prayerful desire and not out of mere curiosity. The most frequent visitors are Muslim women. They visit Lourdes as willingly as they visit Mary's house at Ephesus, or Notre Dame de la Garde, or Our Lady of Africa in Algeria. Mary holds an honoured place in the Qu'ran. She is the only woman called by name: Maryam. There are some twenty passages which speak of her. For the most part they correspond to what the Gospels and Christian Tradition teach about Mary. Apart from naming her as the Mother of Jesus, she is the model for all who believe.

Secondly, at Lourdes Muslims can witness Christians praying and see how they express their prayer through certain attitudes and actions. This greatly helps Islamic-Christian dialogue because for the majority of Muslims, the word "Christian" is synonymous with "the West". If "the West" is ungodly, as certain texts of the Qu'ran would have us believe, then Christians are ungodly.

At Lourdes, Muslims can see Christian men and women praying freely, without being afraid, not enclosed inside a church. In front of the grotto you can find the same open space that you find in a mosque. Our churches are filled with cumbersome chairs and benches: kneeling can be an awkward and uncomfortable gesture. Pilgrims have always been treated with respect by the Eastern Church: no pilgrim has ever been violated in the Holy Land. With this in their favour, shrines like Lourdes can fulfil their particular responsibility: day to day relations, humanitarian cooperation and dialogue.

If we travel to the Far East, we find that here too Mary is venerated. Lourdes still remembers the visit of the Dalai Lama to the grotto on 15 November 1993. He bore a gift of exquisite material to offer to the Blessed Virgin as a token of deep respect and reverence. He was able to compare Mary to Tara the goddess of compassion.

Every year millions of pilgrims flock to Vailankani, the "Lourdes of India". Only a minority are Christians. Mary is mother and so she can understand all our troubles. She is not only compassionate but powerful. She helps all who invoke her. Many Hindus could have adopted the words of St Bernard's prayer "The Memorare" as their own.

Some Christians object to expressions of devotion to Mary, as for them they divinise Mary who, although she is the most perfect of creatures, remains nonetheless a creature. This is not a concern for the Hindus who go to Vailankani, or the Tamils who come to Lourdes. They are quite at ease with more than one divinity.

There is no danger of syncretism and adoring the Goddess–Mother, whilst mixing up mythology, beliefs and traditions from all ages and places. Mary is unique: Israel's most beautiful flower, mother of the Messiah, Mother of God. Just as she is Mother of the New Adam, she is Mother of the whole of humanity which has been saved. To reject the homage paid to her by the faithful of other religions would demonstrate jealousy and narrow-mindedness.

Are the signs at Lourdes universal or specifically Christian?

The message of Lourdes is not only conveyed through words, albeit very few words. It is conveyed by Bernadette's own actions and she was such a convincing witness. It is also conveyed through signs, material and human, almost self-explanatory, that everyone can see and hear as they pass slowly through the shrine: the open air grotto; the spring; the candles; a cosmopolitan crowd; the sick who are surrounded by kindness and care.

The language is universal. In every religion we find water, rock and cave or grotto, light, crowds, the sick and those who serve them. Water is a symbol of life and purity. Rock represents solidity. Beneath its shelter, the cave or grotto, guards secrets. With light we can illuminate the invisible or use it to celebrate feasts. As for the sick and those who care for them, they express the unity of our race, in spite of our physical and linguistic differences.

Because of these universal signs, Lourdes is immediately accessible. Unless someone is totally closed to any spiritual dimension whatsoever, every visitor to Lourdes finds through these signs something to make him a better person. The monuments, the statues, the surroundings all take second place. Whether they are pleasing or not, is not important.

These universal symbols enable everyone to feel at home. They are also deeply biblical, even liturgical. Water is present from the very first chapter of Genesis to the passion of Christ when water flows from his pierced side. Water is the element with which we have been baptised.

The image of the rock symbolises God himself in the Old Testament, and in the New Testament it is the symbol of Peter's faith on which Christ builds his Church, just as the

Basilica of the Immaculate Conception is built upon the rock of Massabielle.

Passing through the grotto is like an Easter journey. Just as Christ descended to the darkest depths of our human condition to rise up again on Easter morning, so too the pilgrim passes through the grotto and emerges on the other side to a mass of burning candles. Symbolically, is not Christ himself the Light and has he not instructed his disciples to be light for the world.

Christ has founded a new humanity from which no people or race is excluded. His message is universal. On the day of Pentecost, his Spirit enabled the apostles to speak in the many different languages of the Jews who were staying in Jerusalem at the time. This is what we hear too in Lourdes.

Christ is present in the sick too, and those who care for them. Two phrases of the Gospel come to mind: "I was sick and you visited me" and "I come among you as one who serves".

At Lourdes, words are secondary. There is little need to explain the Christian significance of the symbols through which God has chosen to reveal himself there. The spirit of Lourdes is the opposite of indoctrination. Freedom of belief is expressed physically through freedom of movement throughout the shrine.

Non-Christians are able to discover the originality of the signs that we hold in common with them, which in Lourdes speak of Christ and the Christian way of life. On one or two special occasions Lourdes is a place of inter-religious dialogue. We would like to make Lourdes always more a place where our Christian origins can be discovered freely.

Inter-religious dialogue

It is not easy to write about inter-religious dialogue at Lourdes. This Marian shrine in the Pyrenees does not hold such a powerful attraction as her counterpart in Portugal. For Muslims, Fatima evokes the name of the prophet Mohammed because his daughter was called Fatima. Some believe that it was even Fatima who appeared and not the Blessed Virgin, making inter-religious dialogue difficult.

Lourdes, however, is not ambiguous. If Muslims and believers of other faiths come to the grotto, it is because of their devotion to Mary. The Second Vatican Council's declaration *Nostra Aetate* indicates that Muslims venerate Jesus as a prophet and honour the Virgin Mary, and at times invoke her. It is a private matter when they come to Lourdes. The most important personality from another religion to come to Lourdes was the

Dalai Lama. During his visit he laid a Tibetan scarf before the statue of the Virgin in the grotto as a sign of deep respect. Buddhists can see in Mary an example of someone without sin, without egoism, an *arhat*, a saint.

My first experience of Lourdes is linked to inter-religious dialogue. I was then 11 years old and I was part of a pilgrimage from the Archdiocese of Birmingham. I was feeling disappointed because I had not been allowed to stay up for the torchlight procession, but the blessing of the sick and the prayers spoken in many languages had profoundly touched me. The idea of becoming a priest had already entered my mind and 18 months later I joined the junior seminary of the African Missionaries (White Fathers).

I was nearly 50 by the time I returned to Lourdes. Everything seemed very different. There were no crowds because it was the month of November. I had been invited to speak to the French bishops during their plenary assembly, on the subject of Muslims in Europe. The other speaker was Father Gilles Couvreur from the French Mission and the Secretariat for Relations with Islam. His task was to analyse Christian-Muslim relations in France. All the talks were part of the preparation process prior to the publication in 1998 of the Bishops' Conference document entitled *Catholics and Muslims: the path to encounter and dialogue*. There were no Muslims present either during our discussion or at the next set of discussions, perhaps because they had not been sufficiently consulted during the preparatory stage. This had not been the case at the special Assembly of the Bishops' Synod on the situation in Lebanon, held in Rome in 1995. On that occasion a large number of representatives from the Sunni, Shiite and Druse communities had been invited to be present as observers.

A few years later I was invited to Lourdes once again. Every year Bishop Jacques Perrier invites the organisers of diocesan pilgrimages to reflect together on the theme chosen for the following year. In November 2003 the theme was centred on the symbolism of the grotto and rock. A special focus was given to the inter-religious dimension of this theme, led by the very talented Christian Solenson, as well as a team of lecturers from the Institute of Science and Theology of Religions in Marseille.

It was of great interest to discover the significance of the grotto or cave in the various religions. The Hindu *sannyasi* or astetic, often sought the silence of the mountain grotto to discover the divine presence deep within him. The *sirah*, or biography of Mohammed, reminds us that at the age of 40, the prophet sought refuge in the cave of al-Hira on the outskirts of Mecca, in order to pray and reflect. According to tradition, it is there that the first few verses of the Qu'ran were inspired. Other caves too play an important role in the story of the *hijra*, Mohammed's escape from Mecca to Medina. In mortal danger at the hands of his enemies, Mohammed and his companion Abu Bakr took refuge in a cave. Tradition says that no one found them because a spider wove her web across the entrance to the cave. We also observed the significance of the rock or stone in many traditions, whether it be the menhirs of Brittany, the monolith Ayers Rock in Australia or the black rock in the Ka'ba in Mecca.

But what importance do all these observations hold for the organisers of pilgrimages? Perhaps they remind us of the underlying human element in every pilgrimage. Human beings were created by God and their destiny is to return to him. It is natural to search for meaning outside oneself. Our distant ancestors were aware of a hidden power, of a Supreme being, at times father-like, and they expressed their awareness in their religious and traditional rituals. When people kneel down in a holy place they are merely doing what others have been doing for centuries before them. When the pilgrims at

Lourdes feel compelled to touch the rock at the grotto of Massabielle, they are behaving in a very human way. They know that power does not come from the rock itself, but its power can be felt because it is a sign of the infinite power of God who is the "Rock of our salvation" (Ps 95, 1).

When we go on a pilgrimage to Lourdes, we melt into the flow of people who down the centuries have sought God in the mountains, forests and rivers in order to return with new strength to their ordinary everyday lives. Why not believe then, that Mary our Mother is leading us to her Son, born in a cave and buried in a cave, but against whom the stone which sealed the entrance could not hold out. In becoming a man, the Son of God took on all that is human, except sin, so as to lead the whole of humanity back to the Father.

+ *Michael L Fitzgerald*
Papal Nuncio, Eygpt.
8 May 2007

CHAPTER TWELVE

THE MISSION OF THE CHURCH
AND THE MARGINALIZED

There is something insensitive even hypocritical about referring to "the marginalized" when one is an integral member of society and the Church. Marginalization takes many forms. The danger is only to focus on a few and not all. For example, marginalization can be a feeling, or how a person perceives a situation – a child may feel out of the family circle, to the despair of its parents, brothers and sisters.

The Church's mission towards the marginalized is often controversial and politically sensitive. At Lourdes however, it would be impossible not to get involved in it, because of Bernadette.

Bernadette, patroness of the marginalized?

Bernadette is not a sweet shepherdess surrounded by fluffy

sheep who sees a beautiful lady. Rather she is surrounded by misery and desolation. To speak about the Church's mission towards the marginalized, we need to begin by looking at the reality of Bernadette's own situation.

In 1858, Bernadette Soubirous' life was not normal, even for a fourteen year-old girl living in Bigorre in the 19th century. Her health was fragile and her asthma attacks led her family to fear the worst; she was a constant worry to them. On 11th February, the day of the first apparition, her mother hesitated sending her out to collect wood with the others. What if she should catch a cold?

Bernadette did not go to school because of her health, and because she had to look after her younger brothers and sisters whilst her mother went out to work to try and earn a few pennies.

The consequences of not going to school meant that Bernadette did not learn French and as a result was not able to attend the parish catechism classes. By 14, she still had not made her first Holy Communion. Bernadette's situation confirms the unhappy fact that one misfortune can often lead to another.

The Soubirous family were poor, but they had not always been so. Advances in technology and the generosity with which they ran their business, forced them to leave "the mill of happiness" at Boly, where Bernadette had been born. Their plight went from bad to worse. François, the father, was no longer his own boss. He had lost an eye and had to take paid work from other millers when they needed him. His wife, Louise, was unable to find work in the fields and had to become a washerwoman.

The family moved from one lodging to another until finally, in November 1856, they came to the former jail, no longer in use because it was too narrow and unfit for human habitation.

At the time of the apparitions then, the Soubirous family were in an extremely precarious situation: managing to feed the children was a daily struggle. One of the boys had been noticed in church scraping up remains of candles to try and earn himself something with which to buy food.

To this already bleak picture, we must also add that the family did not have the best reputation. Financial ruin is even more scandalous than poverty. Bernadette's father was regarded as lazy. He was falsely accused of theft and spent a few days in prison. When Bernadette was later threatened with prison herself, she knew exactly what that meant.

Bernadette's mother had a reputation for drinking. Some of the women in her family, such as Aunt Bernarde and Aunt Basile, were unmarried mothers. The parish priest, Mgr Peyramale must have known the background when Bernadette was brought to his presbytery. He dealt very roughly with this young girl who never came to catechism classes and who was now asking him to hold processions and build a chapel. On 2nd March, weary with all the trouble, he was heard to say "We are very unfortunate to have such a family disturbing the peace of our town."

Bernadette's strong points

The picture was not totally black, however. The Soubirous family were closely united by their love and faith. François chose Louise to be his wife in preference to her elder sister. There were many difficulties including financial ones and above all the loss of several children, but this had not shaken their faith or their love. The family remained strong. Distant relatives helped to support them. The cachot was undoubtedly a desperate measure but it was thanks to a cousin, Sajous, that they were able to move in, and that a meal was waiting for them when they arrived.

When the chief of police, Jacomet, wished to intimidate Bernadette by threatening her with prison, a small crowd gathered outside his office to pray for Bernadette and her father. The incidents were still recent. No miracle had yet occurred. The people could have allowed themselves to be influenced by the chief of police, but they were brave enough to stand up for this young girl, who after all had done nothing wrong: "There is nothing bad about a woman with a rosary."

Bernadette's life indicates several ways in which Lourdes can be a sign. She suffered illness, deprivation, a damaged reputation, lack of education and was not allowed to receive the Eucharist, yet she was able to count on her faith and the support of her family and neighbours.

How can we contribute in each of these areas?

To marginalize people is contrary to the message of the Gospel. Christ came to remove the walls of hatred. The Good News announced to the Ephesians was that they were now "fellow citizens with the holy people of God", no longer guests or outsiders (Ephesians 2, 19).

1 Health

We have spoken in depth in previous chapters about the sick and disabled. It is enough to say here that Bernadette is an example of how problems of health must not be taken in isolation. There are causes and effects. If her conditions in life had not been so wretched, Bernadette's health would have undoubtedly been better. As it was, her poor health affected her education. So, we should always take all the circumstances into consideration.

2 Poverty

There have always been pilgrims who have been unable to afford board and lodging at the shrine. Often, problems of money add to problems of health. This was true in Bernadette's case, and also among the elderly whom the Sisters of Nevers took into their hospice and whom Bernadette learnt to serve, care for and love.

For those with nowhere to stay, Henri Lasserre, successful author of one of the first books published on Lourdes, paid for a large round tent in the area where Our Lady's crowned statue now stand, but the tent was blown down in a storm. Since then a long list of construction work has taken place to fulfil this mission of welcome at Lourdes.

As the Centenary of the apparitions approached, Bishop Théas was aware of a considerable lack of welcome for the poor. He requested Mgr Rodhain, founder of "Secours Catholique", to oversee the organisation of a Centre for the Poor, which could accommodate the poorest pilgrims. On 1st August 1955 the foundation stone was laid and blessed and the building work began for what was to be the St Peter Centre for the Poor, for those pilgrims who most resemble Bernadette in her poverty. Today, it is called "Cité St Pierre", without the word 'poor' so as not to condone poverty.

Since the 1950s, the situation has changed a great deal. The beggar and the tramp used to be a familiar sight at the doors of the church, but they were alone. Today, our society is producing a growing number of people without the security of a family, of a place to live or a job. This is the destructive cycle of many who are marginalized, often involving drugs

163

as well as alcohol. Nowadays many come to beg at the main tourist sites.

Lourdes City Council exercises the right to impose bans or to expel people showing aggressive behaviour or falsely appearing distressed in order to make pilgrims take pity on them. However, we need to recognise that we do not know how to deal very well with this section of society. Some individuals have the special skills needed to communicate with this group and even to give them a new opportunity in life.

If we are so helpless in front of these marginalized people, why do we say that Lourdes has a mission to help them. We can at least encourage pilgrims to remember in their prayers, or daily lives, and perhaps in their future commitments, these brothers and sisters of ours who are so far away from our own standards of living.

3 Poor reputation

One great advantage of the shrine is that the pilgrim can remain anonymous. No one is preceded by his or her reputation. Even groups of people whose behaviour cannot be endorsed, but who are loved by Jesus, are free to come to Lourdes. There are pilgrimages for alcoholics, prostitutes and trans-sexuals. They do not carry a banner but they know that the Church, in one of its most sacred of places, does not reject them. What would be difficult in parish life is possible in Lourdes and this then is part of our mission.

Without confusing the issue, we shall mention a situation which recurs every year: the pilgrimage for "travellers" which celebrates its 50th anniversary this year. It is pointless to hide the fact or paint a rosy picture of these moments which present some problems every year to the local community, all the more because these travellers do not bring any revenue to the town. If an incident occurs, the shrine is immediately held responsible. Whilst seeking to keep the number of incidents to a minimum, the Church has a corresponding evangelical duty to observe: it cannot pronounce a group of people as undesirable.

4 Lack of education

At 14 years of age Bernadette did not know how to read or write. She could not speak French, only her local dialect, as different from one valley to the next; which produced some amusing misunderstandings during her interrogations.

One of the most unjust accusations levelled at the Church is that of wishing to uphold ignorance amongst the masses. The opposite is true; missionaries have always provided clinics and schools. The Sisters of Nevers carried out both these works, long before Bernadette was born. Bernadette herself was unable to benefit from this provision. Our Lady speaks to her heart. She laughs when Bernadette tries to offer her the pencil and paper given to her by Mademoiselle Peyret so that the Lady might write down her name. "There is no need for me to write down what I have to say to you." On one occasion when we are told Jesus wrote something down, he simply traced some markings on the ground, but no one knew what they meant. Our religion is definitely not one that is only read in a book.

The Catholic Church has great respect for the written word. We read Holy Scripture and our present Pope writes books. However, for the many who never open a book, they too have a right to receive the Gospel. For them, Lourdes speaks the language of signs: the rock, the grotto, the spring, the candles, the different languages, the care of the sick, the processions. With good reason one can reproach the Church for being too intellectual and using abstract language. At least at Lourdes this is not the case.

5 Being deprived of the Eucharist

It was Pope Pius X who, in 1910, encouraged children from the age of 7 to receive Holy Communion. At 14 years of age, Bernadette was late making her First Holy Communion. For several reasons Bernadette had not attended the catechism classes. No catechism, no Communion. Yet Bernadette never feels excluded from the Christian community. She prays with her family; she recites the rosary; she goes to Mass and vespers, although we don't know how much she understood. On her second visit to the grotto she took with her some holy water from the parish church in case the apparitions had anything to do with an evil spirit. Each time she returned to Massabielle she carried a candle.

Bernadette's example shows us that Christian life does not only consist of Holy Communion. There are many Christians who do not or cannot receive Communion at Mass, not only those who have been divorced and remarried in a civil ceremony, but also those who feel they have committed grave sins; those who are living with partners, or those who have not yet made their First Holy Communion, or Christians of other traditions.

The Church respects their sincerity, but needs to offer ways in which they can express and nourish their faith. Lourdes has many advantages in this respect; first the pilgrimage itself, visiting the grotto; observing the words of the Blessed Virgin: "Go and drink from the fountain and bathe in the waters"; the Way of the Cross, the Rosary, or simply the silence in front of the grotto amidst other believers, and the procession and adoration of the Blessed Sacrament; a whole range from which the pilgrim is free to choose. And then when darkness falls, pilgrims see each other in the light of their torches as a single family whom Mary looks upon with tenderness.

As we reflect on Bernadette's life, we wonder how she managed with so many disadvantages; but then we remember her faith and the solidarity of her family and neighbourhood. To watch over, to awaken and to nourish faith, this is the first mission of the Church, that which is truly her own. It is also the mission of Lourdes, and has been from the very beginning. Before the apparitions had been approved, Mgr Peyramale, parish priest, noticed increased devotion amongst his parishioners.

What does Lourdes do to reinforce the unity of families and communities? The family dimension has not been emphasized sufficiently. Promises of marriage and reconciliation between couples have certainly taken place at Lourdes, but more is needed to encourage the mixing of generations within the family.

Concerning loneliness, we are indebted to the Welcome Centres which keep in touch with people they have accompanied at Lourdes once they are back at home. We are indebted also to the journeys of hope which the "Cité Saint-Pierre" proposes to the local delegations of "Secours Catholique".

The Church's openness towards the marginalized needs to enlarge and diversify. Lourdes too should play a part in this openness towards our disadvantaged brothers and sisters.

PERSONAL EXPERIENCE

The marginalized

It was Marcella, a transsexual from Argentina, who first had the idea of going on a pilgrimage to Lourdes. "I would like to go to this place Lourdes that I've heard you talk about here," she said, "here" being the "Bois de Boulogne" (one of Paris' most notorious red-light districts).

For the last few years I had been working with the Freedom to Prisoners Association to arrange for a bus to go out three nights a week to meet up with prostitutes, transvestites and transsexuals. "Father," they call to me as they greet me when the bus arrives. We offer them coffee and listen to them, they even ask us to say a prayer before we leave. When we suggested the idea of going to Lourdes, we had no idea what their reaction would be. In the end, for our first pilgrimage in 2003, there was a group of about 20, without Marcella, who had proposed the idea and who was a great believer in retreats and monasteries. The night before leaving I went to say Mass with some of them and I prayed to Our Lady: "Those who come are those who you will take by the hand." We never know exactly who will come, nor their motives which vary from one to the other. On the whole they come because they are touched that someone is thinking of them, others come to take advantage of a free trip.

I remember that first pilgrimage: the excitement as well as the apprehension once we were on the train. For all of us it is an opportunity to go beyond the two hours of friendship we usually spend together at the "Bois de Boulogne". One of the girls mentioned confession, but then laughed and said she would never dare to go. The next day she added, "Unless it is with Father". On the last day she came to me and I reconciled her with God. Vanessa had brought Laura, an Italian friend with her, who used to be a prostitute but who now had Aids and was in a wheelchair. She really enjoyed the change of scene and for two days we made a fuss of her, something she had never experienced before.

Many good things come from these pilgrimages. It is not easy for the women. They come to us weighed down, scarred and battered by life. They often feel second rate and out of place. We offer them lots of different activities. On the first night we go to the pictures, which always proves very popular! As we watch the film Bernadette, by Jean Delannoy, the first tears start to flow. Like them, Bernadette is poor and humble, they are touched by her simplicity. They find in her a very positive image. As their stay unfolds, relationships grow and differences diminish. Something begins to stir. The first time we suggested that they go to the pool, they didn't have much faith in the idea, but then suddenly "Bingo!"

They liked the act of purification, even though for a few, their sexual identity was not very clear and it was not easy to expose their bodies. We were welcomed with great simplicity and generosity by the local team of helpers. They kept one of the pools open out of hours and do the same for us each year. The nuns too who put us up with such hospitality, make it all the more easy to adapt to the new situation; they are always smiling, patient and available. They continued to smile at us even after being woken up in the middle of the night by all our noise. Some of our pilgrims had smoked in their rooms, despite being asked not to. In between prayers at the grotto, Mass and the Way of the Cross, some of them can't resist going shopping in the souvenir shops, which are a great attraction. They are big fans of small statues and medals of all shapes and sizes, which they get blessed. They bring back a lot of water, for themselves, to continue purifying themselves and for those who were not able to come. Even though they find friendships difficult, they are touched and want to share what they have felt at Lourdes.

Going home is painful - no one wants to go back. They feel anguished and so do we, as we know that they are going back to their life in the Bois, sometimes that same night. We try to prolong our time at the station by having a sandwich and a coffee, but no one comes to meet them.

We think of Jennifer and pray for her. She was 25 when she managed to get out of her situation. After having been a prostitute from the age of 14, this transsexual girl gave it up and now lives in Toulon where she is studying to become a children's magistrate. Lourdes touched her. She had received a copy of the Gospels from the Bishop which she had read and re-read, overwhelmed that someone had given her a gift. The friendship and trust that she had built up with Michèle, one of our helpers, helped her find peace in her childlike heart.

Some of them have hearts of gold, their souls are as innocent as children's. I remember being very moved by a question from one of them on our return, "It's very sweet of you to think of us, but are there any other Catholics as kind as you who will look after others. You know, the people who come to see us in the Bois are very unhappy, they need God too."

Fr Jean Philippe
Community of St John

CONCLUSION

LOURDES TODAY

Building work has been a permanent feature in Lourdes since the beginning. At first it was the barricades ordered by the Mayor to keep people out of the grotto, barricades that were put up during the day only to be taken down at night by the same people who had put them up. Soon, however, more serious work began to be undertaken by the "Bishop of the apparitions" Mgr Laurence. Even before the apparitions had been officially approved, the bishop had begun to acquire surrounding land in order to protect the grotto and to carry out the request of the Blessed Virgin to build a chapel.

Since then, building work has been almost non-stop. A record of the construction work has been kept by Canon Courtin and more recently by P. Branthomme and Chantal Touvet.

The buildings are a message in themselves. They include churches, welcome centres and bridges, constituting a wonderful programme for Lourdes and a wonderful symbol for the Church itself: churches in which to pray and celebrate the Eucharist; welcome centres because the Gospel needs to be announced to everyone, called to be one family; bridges within and outside the shrine, because we must work for peace and unity both within and outside the Church.

By fulfilling the 12 missions outlined in this book, we are building churches, welcome centres, and bridges in our world. Then there is the book that still needs to be written, which could be entitled the "Lourdes of Tomorrow?" with a question mark, because God is always free to change his plans in keeping with the times. For the moment at least it would seem that he does not want it to be become a museum!

Even today, as I write this post script, looking ahead to this Sunday for example, the Church will celebrate the Eucharist which Bernadette so desired and loved, but also, as well as the usual flow of pilgrims who make up the heart of Lourdes, five of the newest groups to Lourdes will be present: the sick who need dialysis; those involved in alcoholic recovery; or concerned with the care of prostitutes; motorcycle police, able-bodied and disabled sports men and women.

For various reasons, these people may think that they are far from the Church or that the Church is far from them. Welcoming them, either discreetly or visibly, is an honour and a wonderful responsibility for Lourdes. These initiatives have only come about over the last 5 years. Lourdes is rich in many, as yet unexplored possibilities, as is the Church herself. Beneath this wide mantle, Mary welcomes all those who turn to her.